Francis D Clark

The First Regiment of New York Volunteers

Commanded by Col. Jonathan D. Stevenson, in the Mexican War...

Francis D Clark

The First Regiment of New York Volunteers
Commanded by Col. Jonathan D. Stevenson, in the Mexican War...

ISBN/EAN: 9783337010300

Printed in Europe, USA, Canada, Australia, Japan

Cover: Foto ©ninafisch / pixelio.de

More available books at **www.hansebooks.com**

Your Friend & Servt
J. D. Thomson

1846—1882.

THE FIRST REGIMENT

OF

NEW YORK VOLUNTEERS

COMMANDED BY

COL. JONATHAN D. STEVENSON,

IN THE MEXICAN WAR.

NAMES OF THE MEMBERS OF THE REGIMENT DURING ITS TERM OF SERVICE IN UPPER AND LOWER CALIFORNIA, 1847-1848, WITH A RECORD OF ALL KNOWN SURVIVORS ON THE 15TH DAY OF APRIL, 1882, AND THOSE KNOWN TO HAVE DECEASED, WITH OTHER MATTERS OF INTEREST PERTAINING TO THE ORGANIZATION AND SERVICE OF THE REGIMENT.

COMPILED BY THEIR COMRADE,

FRANCIS D. CLARK.

New York:
GEO. S. EVANS & CO., PRINTERS, 38 CORTLANDT STREET.
— 1882 —

NOTE.

The names recorded in this work have been furnished by GENERAL R. C. DRUM, Adjutant-General of the Army, from the official rolls of the regiment on file in the WAR DEPARTMENT. The record appended to each name has been prepared with great care, notwithstanding which inaccuracies may be discovered. Those *survivors* to which an * is attached, the information was derived directly from themselves by letter or personal interview—to those reported *deceased*, the date and place of death is given, where the information could be obtained ; in all cases where the State is not designated, the place mentioned is in California. Comrades in perusing the rolls are particularly requested to report any error or information omitted.

F. D. C.

INTRODUCTION.

· COMRADES:

In presenting this Liliputian volume no apology is offered. It contains all the information and facts possible in a space of necessity limited by the funds contributed therefor by a few of our comrades. You will find, however, a record that may prove interesting and valuable to all—*the names of those who served in the regiment during its term of service in California*, a record of those *known* to be living, also of those *known* to have deceased. This information, while not as complete as desired, has been acquired during a period of eleven years, requiring over one thousand written communications, and the distribution, during that period, of some fifteen hundred printed circulars and postal cards addressed to comrades, involving labor and expense of which this little waif fails to give the reader an adequate idea; the labor, however, was one of love, and I trust it may prove an acceptable offering to my surviving comrades and their friends.

Thirty-five years have elapsed since our regiment landed on the soil of California, and over thirty-three years have passed since the Government dispensed with our services, leaving each member of the regiment free from further military service, and thereafter to assume the responsibility of citizenship, each for himself to carve out his own future. In one respect we were favored beyond any other regiment serving during the Mexican war, in being discharged in California the same year that gold was discovered at Sutter's saw-mill, but a few months subsequent to that event, and it is to be regretted that so few of us are enjoying the benefits resulting from that wonderful discovery. Yet it is a question whether that discovery was not as unfortunate for ourselves, as it proved to be for many others in the country, including that noble old pioneer, General John A. Sutter, through whose instrumentality the discovery was made. Is it not a matter of fact, that it somewhat rudely invaded happy homes, and interrupted the peaceful, prosperous, and contented lives then being led by the native population of California.

I will make no attempt to lay before you the difficulties experienced in obtaining the information presented in these pages. The long period that elapsed since the discharge of the regiment, had erased from the memory of the majority of our comrades the recollection of events, many died within a few years subsequent to their discharge from the service, many were scattered to remote parts of the world, and too many were disinclined to take up the pen to transmit a record of what their memory may have retained, but others freely contributed such information as they possessed or could obtain.

My own experience regarding the surviving members of the regiment has undoubtedly been that of others. In 1870— when I first entered upon this self-imposed task—I knew of only two other members of the regiment living in New York— notwithstanding my having been engaged in business there for the fifteen years prior to that date, I ascertained that during that time twelve others were also residents of the city; but considering the fact that the members of the regiment were conveyed to California in six transports, and while in California were stationed in eight towns, it is not to be wondered that to a great extent they were almost strangers to each other, many acquaintances being formed subsequent to their discharge from the service.

A homely but familiar adage says: "Self praise is no recommendation;" all that is given in these pages in commendation of our old organization comes from those who were in nowise connected therewith; and from that evidence may our fellow-citizens judge of its character; to these impartial critics may we safely entrust our record, which now forms part of the history of our beloved country.

In 1871, and again in 1874, you were furnished with a pamphlet giving the result of my researches up to those dates. With this publication I bring my labors to a close, trusting they have not been altogether in vain; should they be the means of renewing old acquaintance, after so long a separation, or of reviving old associations of those eventful days, I shall feel amply repaid for the time and labor expended thereon.

In conclusion, I beg to tender my sincere thanks for the courtesy, kindness and assistance granted to me by the Hon. Robert T. Lincoln, Secretary of War—General William T. Sherman, U. S. A.—who, having served contemporaneous with us in California, has upon many occasions in late years exhibited his friendship for the members of our regiment—Gen. R. C. Drum, Adjutant General U. S. Army, Col. Jonathan D. Stevenson, (our Colonel), Col. Thomas C. Lancey, and John Q. Adams, Esq., and to the press of the Golden State.

FRANCIS D. CLARK,
Late Co. D, First Regt., N. Y. Vols.

RETROSPECT.

In 1846, the year war was declared between the United States and Mexico, the question of a journey to the Territory of California, was one for no little consideration, as it seemed somewhat like being exiled from the civilized world; and in those days few had occasion or desire to visit that distant land; whether the choice was a voyage by sea or overland the time required to reach Yerba Buena, now San Francisco, was from five to six months. A few Americans were residents of the country at that time, having found their way there by vessels trading for hides and on whaling voyages; others following the course of the setting sun across the plains, scaling the Rocky Mountains and the Sierra Nevada, found themselves upon the Pacific coast, and becoming infatuated with the life of ease and plenty afforded by its delightful climate, and the opportunity of securing a livelihood with little or no toil, by engaging in stock-raising, they were influenced in making California their home. For a time Americans were highly esteemed by the native Californians, and, with rare exception, received with the warmest hospitality. In a few years, however, the Mexican officials began to look upon the Americans with jealousy and suspicion, and to assume an attitude of hostility, so serious, indeed, that on the 14th day of June, 1846, the Americans banded themselves together for self-protection under the celebrated "Bear Flag," and had not the declaration of war between the two countries been proclaimed at the time it was, open hostilities would soon have waged between the American settlers and the Mexican forces on duty in the territory.

Early in the summer of 1846, President Polk decided upon sending a force of volunteers by sea to the Pacific Coast, also Co. F of the 3d U. S. Artillery, by the U. S. storeship Lexington. Among the lieutenants of this company were the present General of the Army, William T. Sherman, and General E. O. C. Ord, U. S. A.; also the late General Henry W. Halleck, then captain in the engineer corps. General **Stephen W. Kearny** was ordered to proceed overland with a squadron of dragoons, via New Mexico. Captain **John C. Fremont, with a surveying party**, having arrived in California during the month of January, 1846, **remained** upon the soil of Mexico with his small command, no **doubt under** the instructions of our Government, and upon the outbreak of hostilities took a very prominent part. These movements on the part of the army were for the purpose of taking possession of and holding California, with a view to its acquisition on the cessation of difficulties between the two countries. Mr. Polk little suspected what a store of wealth he was securing to the future benefit of his country when he conceived this purpose, for scarcely two years elapsed ere the discovery of gold at Sutter's Saw-mill proclaimed to the world that the El Dorado had been found within the domain of our great Republic; wealth for centuries laid hidden, had now been revealed through the **indomitable** spirit of progress, civilization, and enterprise which ever follows the footsteps of the American pioneers of the West. **Nearly thirty-six years** have elapsed since President Polk directed **the organization** of that regiment of volunteers in the Empire State for duty in California; a body selected with great care, the intention of the Government being that these volunteers, the majority of whom were under twenty-one years of age, should be discharged in that country at the close **of the war, thus forming** a colony, around which would **cluster Americans** then in the country, as well as those who would afterwards **find** their way to that distant land in search of homes. Many Americans had already settled in the neighboring territory of Oregon, and attention was being drawn to California, not simply on account of its fine climate, but in anticipation of it soon becoming the property of our own Government.

This regiment of New York Volunteers was organized in 1846, under the direction of Jonathan D. Stevenson, a gentleman whose subsequent administrative ability proved his eminent fitness for the position, and upon assembling on Governor's Island, New York harbor, he became its colonel. On the 26th day of September, 1846, the regiment sailed for its destination in the ships "Thomas H. Perkins," "Susan Drew," and "Loo Choo," followed a few months later by the ships "Brutus," "Isabella," and "Sweden," with additional men to fill up the command. Few of those now residents of the Empire City and State have any recollection of the youthful and hardy band that sailed from their State to play so important a part in the organization and settlement of a then far-off country. What a contrast between the California of 1846 and that of 1882!—then an almost unknown and sparsely settled Mexican territory; now one of the constellation of States, teeming with populous cities and enterprising, industrious, law-abiding citizens—then it required 180 days to make the tedious, tiresome voyage between New York and San Francisco, now it is performed with ease and pleasure in six days and a few hours.

The discovery of gold at Sutter's Mill in 1848, caused the rapid influx of thousands upon thousands, by sea and land, not only from the Atlantic States, but from all parts of the globe, thereby adding largely to the population (floating, in a great measure) of California. Towns sprang up in every portion of the mountains comprising the mining regions, and thus these volunteers, destined by the Government to be the nucleus of the settlement of this remote land, were almost insensibly absorbed by the masses then rapidly pouring into the country. Yet this body of early pioneers has contributed some of California's most enterprizing and worthy citizens, and during the late civil war many of them proved their patriotic devotion to their country, filling honorable and distinguished positions as generals, colonels, and other officers in the volunteer army.

In this little volume are recorded the names of all who were members of the regiment while on duty in California,—March 6th, 1847, to October 26th, 1848—showing who were living on the 15th day of April, 1882, also those known to have deceased prior to that date, with other matters of interest pertaining to the organization known as the " First Regiment of New York Volunteers," commanded by Col. Jonathan D. Stevenson, in the service of the United States during the Mexican war.

In connection with the organization and fitting out of the regiment during the summer of 1846, the following editorials from the *New York Herald*, presents the facts and incidents in a clear and concise shape, and, from the impartial character of that journal, truthfulness may be relied upon.

From the Herald of August 3, 1846.

Its issue of August 3, 1846, says—" We yesterday paid a visit to Governor's Island for the purpose of seeing if the good reports given of the body of volunteers there, soon to embark for California, were true; indeed, we were agreeably surprised in finding everything so different from what we expected in a number of men so lately collected together. They are encamped on the south-western side of the island, and their new white tents, pitched with military supervision presented a fine appearance. There are now on the ground eight companies, comprising about 600 men, which will be increased to the full regimental number of 770 by the arrival of two companies from the interior of the state. In watching the men as they stood in line we could not but notice the excellent material composing them. Some companies, indeed, are like picked men; strong, able-bodied mechanics generally, in prime of life, and already somewhat schooled in the discipline of the service. The officers of the regiment are gentlemen of high abilities, and well qualified for their task. Colonel Stevenson's enterprising character is well known. Lieut.-Col. Henry S. Burton, Major James A. Hardie, Captains Shannon and Folsom, are all graduates of West Point, and have till lately held professorships at that institution. Lieut.-Col. Burton is a talented and experienced officer, and Major Hardie is a gentleman who, though always using necessary decision, will endear himself to the soldiers by the kindness of his disposition. The Adjutant of the regiment, Lieutenant Stevenson, a son of the Colonel, is a graduate of West Point, and is every inch a soldier. The uniform of the regiment will soon be completed, designed by Major Hardie, is very neat and serviceable; pantaloons of dark, mixed grey, with scarlet strip or cord up the seam of the leg, blue coats with scarlet trimmings, a new style of French cap, **very becoming**; the first dress parade of the regiment will take place next Sunday. One company, under command of Captain Seymour G Steele, is composed entirely of temperance men. If this body of **men, under** such officers, and of such stamina themselves, do **not create a new state** of things in the region to which they go, we **are much** mistaken. Success attend them."

From the Herald of August 4, 1846.

"A company from Steuben county, under command of Captain Shannon, a fine looking body of men, belonging to the regiment of volunteers on Governor's Island, arrived in this city yesterday."

From the Herald of September 6, 1846.

"THE CALIFORNIA EXPEDITION ITS OBJECT AND PURPOSE. —The preparations and outlay for this expedition have been the cause of much noise, speculation and vituperation among certain portions of the community, who have echoed the half-fledged opinions of a few presses whose conductors have no souls of sympathy with any movement, however advantageous to the country at large, unless it yields directly to the glorification of their peculiar party.

"Again and again it is asked, what is the object of this expedition? and more particularly now, as the war is supposed to be virtually at an end, and the country to which it is destined is really in the possession of the United States. Briefly as possible we will give our ideas of the objects, intended operations and advantages of this expedition.

"The rich and beautiful region of California will without doubt come into formal possession of the United States, without any further fighting for it. Far removed as it is from our seat of Government, inhabited in a measure by a half-civilized people, it will be absolutely necessary, if we intend to hold it, that military possession be taken of it, and that a territorial government be established there, and what is the class who, under such circumstances, are best fitted to do this? Not mere soldiers, whose only knowledge is a military one. Not politicians, who can theorize most beautifully, but whose schemes burst like gas-bubbles when tried by the fire of practice; but the sound, hardy mechanics of our country—the men whose hands know useful labor—the artizan, at whose touch the rough metal is moulded into implements of use—the men who transform the material into the necessaries and luxuries of human existence. The hard-handed, honest laborer, the farmer, the blacksmith, the tailor, the shoemaker, the hatter, the carpenter, the mason; these are men under whose auspices a country rich in soil, healthy in climate, and possessing local advantages of a rare nature, will grow up and flourish. Precisely of this class are the men whom our Government are about sending to California. Nearly every man in the regiment is a mechanic, and may carry his implements of trade with him. Should the regiment be disbanded immediately upon its arrival, it contains within itself the elements of prosperity, wealth and greatness. A great harmony of feeling exists between both officers and men, and a fortnight more will probably find these pioneers in the cause of the advancement of human freedom, civilization and prosperity, on their way to the land of their hopes and future prospects. Arrived there, they will cause the '*wilderness to bud and blossom as the rose tree,*' and plant the standard of the American Government and enterprise upon the soil of California."

From the Herald of September 14, 1846.

"The troops comprising the expedition for the conquest, settlement, or annexation of California, will, in a few days, embark for their destination; and in spite of all the difficulties and opposition attending their progress from the commencement, they will sail, admirably adapted for the purposes intended by the Government to be effected. If their path in a foreign country is to be cut by the sword, strong minds guide and strong arms carry the weapons with which to overcome all obstacles. If they are to settle down quietly in the posssession of the soil, there are hands used to toil, and implements of husbandry and mechanism are ready to be devoted to the improvement of the ground they occupy. In either case, whether their cause is to be one of conquest and just retaliation or of peaceful occupation, the expedition is composed of material well provided with men and means, and one that will do credit to the State which is honored in the selection of her sons for the first body of troops sailing from the United States to a foreign land.

"Much has been said, and much unjustly, relative to the organization of the regiment, and many have been the sneering remarks thrown out, predicting that a corporal's guard would be all remaining, by the time that the day appointed for embarkation came round. The present actual condition and force of the regiment is the best answer to all such aspersions. Ten companies, the full complement of the force, show a muster roll of over 700 men, being as many as are allowed to enlist; a band of excellent musicians is organized; the ships to convey the troops to their destination are chartered, prepared, and ready for sea; a powerful armament of cannon, guns, mortars, and, in fact, of every thing necessary for either a regiment of dragoons, artillery, or infantry has been furnished; clothes, provisions, and necessary equipments of every sort have been provided. The men themselves are contented and anxious to start; the officers generally are men of military knowledge and experience—some of them, and indeed all of the field officers, with the exception of the colonel, have held situations as professors at West Point, which is the best evidence of their fitness for the duties assigned them; and now that this whole body of American citizens, mechanics, and farmers, commanded by able men, are about to go from among us, it is wrong that any of the press of the State which calls them her own, should endeavor to mar the good results and good feeling to be derived from their effects, on account of political or personal prejudice against one or more of the officers.

"Col. Stevenson, who commands the expedition, has a most admirable opportunity of displaying his perseverance and fitness of character to enter upon a bold enterprise, from the commencement of the organization of the regiment up to the present time; probably there are but few men in the country who could design and carry through a project so complicated, and in as successful a manner as he has done. Attacked on every side by political enemies, or disappointed for an approach to the rank which he holds; retarded by the non-action of the Governor of this State, who seems, for some private reasons, to have granted unwillingly and but by degrees, the aid which his station enabled him to afford; encumbered with the supervision and necessary discipline of 700 or 800 men unused to restraint of any kind, he has displayed an energy and boldness which qualify him in a supereminent degree for a commander of a body of troops, which departs upon a business requiring the utmost acumen and perseverance. To Colonel Stevenson, and to his Lieutenant-Colonel, Major, and Adjutant, the whole credit is due for carrying to a prosperous crisis an expedition fraught with interest to every American citizen.

"We say nothing of the ultimate results to be effected from this expedition. The United States Government is fully aware of their importance, judging from the liberal manner in which all necessary outfits have been granted, and we can but wish them that success which seems almost certain to arise from the elements composing their power. We have perfect confidence in the judgment and skill of the superior officers; and as for the men, they are, and all must have, too much at heart the honor of their country ever to disgrace her flag. The fifteen or twenty of them that took advantage of the baby act and left the regiment, could well be spared—their places were filled by better men, and at a future day we hope that the expedition which is soon to sail, will, by their deeds of honor, acquire a name which no one would be unwilling to have bestowed upon himself."

From the Herald of September 29, 1846.

REFERRING TO THOSE WHO HAD BEEN LEFT BEHIND BY THE SHIPS, the issue of **September 29,** 1846, says—" According to notice, a meeting was held yesterday, in the Trophy Room connected with the City Armory, of those who were left behind attached to the California regiment. Captain Nelson Taylor, of Co. E, was confined to his bed by sickness. Lieutenant Geo. F. Penrose, of Co. A, presided, and Lieutenant Thos. L. Vermule acted as secretary. After some remarks from the secretary, he read a letter from Colonel Bankhead, who, as soon as he heard of the situation of those who were prevented sailing, immediately offered to supply them with rations and quarters on the Island till he could hear from the Adjutant-General at Washington; a letter was also read from the daughter-in-law of Secretary (War) Marcy, and wife of the commissary of the regiment, containing information of a cheering character. The secretary stated that those who wished to follow the fortunes of their companions in arms to California would undoubtedly have an opportunity of shortly joining them, as a fast vessel would undoubtedly be dispatched which would overtake the convoy at Rio Janeiro. A series of resolutions were then read and passed unanimously. The purport of them declared their own regret and distress at being left behind. That they wished to join the regiment as soon as possible; that they returned their thanks to Col. Bankhead, and would immediately proceed to the Island; that they had been legally enlisted, and, detesting the name of deserter, would serve their country even as they had sworn to do. Thereupon the whole body, consisting of two lieutenants, four sergeants, and about thirty privates. took up their line of march to the Battery. The whole affair was an excellent comment on those who through the columns of the press have stated that so many were dissatisfied and would desert the first opportunity. These men, one and all, were anxious by any means or in any way to place themselves under the command of Col. Stevenson, in whom their confidence has never been impaired."

After remaining upon Governor's Island some six weeks, the little band of stragglers embarked on board the ship 'Brutus,' Captain Adams, which vessel had been chartered by the Government for that purpose, as also to convey a cargo of stores to California for the use of the command, and on the 13th of November sailed from the port of New York for their destination.

*From the **Herald** of November 13, 1846.*

"The ship which was to have sailed yesterday for the Pacific with Government stores, etc., and having on board those of Col. Stevenson's California Regiment who were left behind on the departure of the main body in September last will sail this day.

"We have received the following card, with a request for its publication, which we comply with, especially as it evinces a proper feeling for a most gallant officer

"'SHIP BRUTUS—NEW YORK HARBOR,
"'November 12, 1846.

"'The undersigned, a committee on behalf of the detachment of the California Regiment, who sail this day for their destination, (with the approbation of their officer,) would seize the only opportunity that occurs of tendering to Col. Bankhead, Commanding at Governor's Island, the grateful acknowledgements, for the kind treatment received by them since the departure of the expedition.

"'The undersigned on behalf of their comrades, while expressing their gratitude, indulge the hope that Col. Bankhead may long enjoy health, and the good will of the citizens of New York.

"' JAMES QUEEN, 1st Sergt., Co. F.
"' AB'M VAN RIPER, 1st Sergt. Co. E.
"' J. S. BALDWIN, 1st Corp., " I.
"' JOHN ROSE, " " G.
"' TYNMAN UPSON, Private, " G.
"' J. E. NUTTMAN, " " B.'

"This we believe is the conclusion of the after piece, following the great drama of the formation and sailing of the California Expedition, as far as this port is concerned. When we next hear from them, may it be from the soil to which they are destined, and of conduct, whether as citizens or soldiers, creditable to the city from which they went forth."

IN the Spring of 1847, Captain James M. Turner, of Co. B, who sailed in the ship "Thomas H. Perkins," at the time the expedition took its departure, having left the vessel upon its arrival at Rio Janeiro, returned to New York City, and upon the authority of the War Department commenced the enlistment of a detachment of two hundred men as recruits for the regiment, and which men, it was announced, would proceed overland to California, but it was subsequently determined that they also should proceed to California by the same route as the expedition. The detachment was stationed at Fort Hamilton, opposite the Narrows of New York Harbor, and on the 16th day of August, 1847, one hundred of the men embarked for Philadelphia, under the command of Lieut. Thomas J. Roach, accompanied by Lieut. John S. Norris, and upon arrival at Philadelphia, the ship "Isabella" (which was ready for sea, and only awaited the arrival of the detachment), received the men on board, and on the following day sailed down the Delaware on her long voyage.

The second detatchment of one hundred men, under command of Lieut. Thomas E. Ketchum, sailed from New York some weeks after the departure of the "Isabella," on board the ship "Sweden." These two vessels reached California in February, 1848.

This new accession filled up the regiment to nearly 900 men; Companies E and G received a portion of the recruits, but the greater portion upon their arrival in Alta-California were sent to Lower California, and assigned to Companies A, B and D.

In the month of March, 1847, the transports "Thomas H. Perkins," "Susan Drew," and "Loo Choo," arrived at San Francisco, and the following month the "Brutus" put in an appearance, and in the month of February, 1848, the "Isabella" and "Sweden" arrived at Monterey. The average voyage of these vessels was 165 days, and with one exception, the vessels touched at South American ports, thereby relieving the monotony of the long and tedious voyage. The health of the men remained good on those vessels that visited ports on the eastern and western coasts of South America, as they were amply provisioned with fresh supplies of vegetables in each port, and the evil effects of the salt provisions furnished at sea was in a measure counteracted, and even the health of those who were aboard the "Brutus," which vessel made no port between New York and San Francisco, remained good until within a few weeks of the termination of the voyage,

At the date of the arrival of the regiment the whole of Upper California was in the possession of the United States authorities, naval and military combined, and among the officers of the army were the present General W. T. Sherman, Major-General Edw. O. C. Ord, as also the late Major-General H. W. Halleck, Lieutenants in the regular service. Upon the arrival of the regiment it was assigned by companies to various portions of the country for the purpose of holding possession and maintaining order under military rule.

In the Spring of 1848 gold was discovered by Marshal, at Sutter's Mill, (Coloma), and although the temptation of earning hundreds of dollars per day in the mines instead of the twenty-three cents received from the Government was almost irresistible, still, to the honor of the command, few were the number who deserted, preferring an *Honorable Discharge* and EMPTY POCKETS to the *golden nuggets* and a *branded name*.

The Fall of that year witnessed the disbandment of the organization, the last companies discharged were A, B and D, at Monterey, on the 24th of October, by Captain Henry S. Burton, 3d U. S. Artillery, (late Lieut.-Col. of the regiment), and Major Henry Hill, Paymaster U. S. Army, having liquidated the claims of both officers and privates, preparations were immediately inaugurated for the departure to the mines. Oxen, carts of the Mexican pattern, horses, mules, saddles, etc., were in great demand, and all in the market found ready purchasers at liberal prices. The distance to the mines at that date (Mokelumne Hill) was about 250 miles, and it was necessary to transport the provisions required for the winter, as the prospect of procuring them at the mines were uncertain, and even if they were to be purchased, the amount required to provide a person with subsistence until they were enabled to perfect their plans for digging would soon deplete their already limited purses.

The writer passed the winter of 1848–9 on the Mokelumne river, about one mile below the hill, and the subjoined were some of the prices demanded and paid for clothing, provisions, &c., in that locality:

Flour, per lb.............	$1 00	Blankets, per pair.......	$ 50 00
Sugar "	2 00	Flannel shirts..........	25 00
Coffee "	3 00	Common boots, per pair	100 00
Pepper in grain per lb.....	5 00	" shoes, "	32 00
Salt pork "	5 00	Mexican serapas (shawls)	100 00
Salt "	1 00		

And a mixture, denominated brandy, whiskey, or gin, of the vilest quality, was retailed at $2 per drink, or $20 per bottle. Canned oysters (one pound), $16 The yield of gold being liberal, these prices were cheerfully paid by the dwellers in the mountains.

As incredible as the above prices may appear they are nevertheless strictly true.

The discovery of gold in California opened up a field of labor and profit which amply repaid the volunteers for their long separation from friends and home in that then far-off distant land, yet 'tis sad to contemplate how few of those adventurous youths and brave pioneers benefited themselves as they had the opportunity offered. A few are at this day (1882) wealthy, but the majority of the survivors are little more than earning a livelihood, and there are, no doubt, among them some who are in destitute circumstances, but the greater part of the men who were discharged in 1848 have ceased to exist, except in the memory of their old comrades and others who in California's early days were numbered among her pioneers.

At the present date the old organization has nearly passed from memory except as one of its former members is borne to the grave, and then his name is mentioned, and on the morrow forgotten, but let us hope that Caifornia's early pioneers, those men and women who wended their way over the rugged mountains or the trackless ocean ere the alluring temptation of gold was presented, may ever live in the history of the Golden State.

ROLL.

Field Officers.

Survivor April 15th, 1882.

*Col. JONATHAN D. STEVENSON .. .. .. San Francisco.
 U. S. Shipping Commissioner at S. F. since 1872.

Deceased.

Lieut. Col. HENRY S. BURTON :. At Fort Adams, R. I., April 4th, '69.
 Major General of Vols. late war.
Major JAMES A. HARDIE .. .. Washington, D. C., Dec. 14th, '76.
 Brig. General of Vols. late war.

Staff Officers.

Survivors, April 15th, 1882.

*Surgeon ALEXANDER PERRY .. New York City.
Ass't Surg. ROBERT MURRAY .. U. S. Army.
 "   "   WILLIAM C. PARKER . .. Oakland, Cal.
Capt. WILLIAM G. MARCY, Commissary .. .. .. Alameda, Cal.
 Secretary State Constitutional Convention at Monterey, 1849.
*Lieut. J. C. BONNYCASTLE, Adjutant .. .. Louisville, Ky.
 Officer of the Regular Army from Oct. 1848 to May 1861.

Deceased.

Capt. JOSEPH L. FOLSOM, A. Q. M. At San Jose Mission, July 15th, '55.

Non-Commissioned Staff.

Deceased.

Sergt.-Major ALEX. C. McDONALD .. Near Cloverdale, April 5th, '80.
Q. M. Sergt. STEPHEN HARRIS .. .. Sep. 26th, '46 to Aug. 12th, '47.
 Date and Place unknown.
Q. M. Sergt. GEORGE G. BELT .. .. Aug. 12th, '47 to July 1st, '48.
 Died at Stockton in 1869.
Q. M. Sergt. JAMES C. LOW .. .. July 1st, '48 to Oct. 26th, '48.
 Died at San Rafael in 18——.

Regimental Band.

Whereabouts Unknown.

COHN, MORITZ	HEHN, HENRY
DUNITCH, ERNEST F.	KRAUSS, CHARLES
ECKER, JOHN	KLEINBROTH, JOHN
ESCHERICK, CARL	MARX, ERNEST
FETZCHOROR, CHRISTIAN	MOSSIA, ANTONIO
FAUFTER, JOHANN	ROANE, JOHN
HUCHAS, HEINRICH	WEHLER, EDWARD
HAUFF, ERNEST	YOUNG, CHARLES D.

Deceased.

*Drum Major GEORGE BATCHELOR
Chief Musician, JOSEPH VEVIS .. Sept. 26th, '46 to Dec. 20th, '47.
" FREDERIC GRAMBIS Dec. 23d, '47 to Oct. 26th, '48.
Date and Place of Death, of above three unknown.
Musician ANTON ROSENTIEL .. At San Francisco, April 4th, '55.
" JOHN WHALEN .. .. At Los Angeles, Dec. 7th, '53.

Sutlers' Department.

Survivor, April 15th, 1882.

*JAMES C. L. WADSWORTH, clerk .. San Francisco.
2d Alcalde of Stockton, 1849.

Deceased.

SAMUEL W. HAIGHT, sutler

Co. "A"

Was recruited by Seymour G. Steele, at "Stoneall's Hotel," on Fulton Street, near Nassau Street, in the City of New York. The first recruits were enrolled on the evening of the 6th of July, 1846. Early on the morning of the 1st of August, the men formed at this rendezvous and took up their line of march for the foot of Whitehall Street, *en route* for Governor's Island. The Battery was thronged by thousands of citizens to witness the departure of the men, who were to compose the "California Expedition" from the city. On the 2d of September the men were sworn and mustered into the service of the United States. On the 23d of September, the Company embarked on board the ship "Loo Choo," which sailed for California three days later, arriving at San Francisco on the 26th day of March, 1847, six months to a day from New York. On the 31st of March the Company embarked on board the bark "Moscow," accompanied by Companies "B" and "F," and sailed for Santa Barbara, at which place they landed on the 8th of April. They encamped on the beach for several days, before going to their barracks in the town of Santa Barbara. On the 4th of July this Company and Company "B" embarked on board the U. S. Storeship "Lexington," and sailed for La Paz, Lower California, a port on the Gulf of California, at which place the Company landed on the 21st of July, 1847. While in the Lower Country, Companies "A" and "B" withstood a siege of some thirty days at La Paz by the Mexican Forces doing duty in Lower California, and upon the arrival of the ship "Isabella" with Company "D" and 114 recruits, in March, 1848, the whole command, under Lieutenant-Colonel Burton, marched into the interior and dispersed the Mexican forces, which outnumbered the Americans five to one. On the 31st day of August, 1848, the Company embarked on board the U. S. Ship of the Line, "Ohio," and sailed September 1st for Monterey, stopping at San Jose, del Cabo, near Cape San Lucas for Company "D," and on the 14th of October following arrived in Monterey, Upper California.

Comrade William H. Rogers of Company "A," under date of Brooklyn, N. Y., December 6th, 1881, in writing his experiences while in the Army, says :

"After a pleasant sail down the Coast, in the Storeship "Lexington," in the month of July, 1847, we rounded the Needle Rocks, off Cape St. Lucas, passed San Jose, and were soon coasting up the Gulf of California, and on July 21st entered the Harbor of La Paz, and came to anchor two miles off shore. Towards sunset we commenced to land in boats. When within three-quarters of a mile of the shore, we took to the water, which was about four feet deep, and waded ashore, with our clothes, muskets and accoutrements on our shoulders. One of our number had his foot badly cut by a pearl shell. After reaching the beach we put on our clothes and fell into line. Captain Steele inquired for the Quartel, and he either mistook the answer or some wag gave him the wrong directions, for in a short time we halted in front of the village grave-yard ; but we were soon righted and about-face for the Quartel, which we reached toward twilight ; found it to be a dilapidated old ruin, full of dirt, fleas and vermin, but the boys soon scattered around the town, leaving only the guard in full possession. Next morning discovered a closet full of wooden stocks for the head, arms and legs, with iron manacles, chains and hand-cuffs. We soon destroyed these relics of barbarism and tyranny by making a good bon-fire of the wooden stocks, and destroying the manacles, chains and cuffs."

Co. "A."

Survibors, April 13th, 1882.

*Capt. SEYMOUR G. STEELE	San Diego.
BARTHROP, EDWARD	San Francisco.
CAHILL, MARTIN	Stockton.
*CLAMP, RICHARD	Chinese Camp.
DENKERS, CHARLES W.	Sacramento.
*DEAN, GILBERT E.	Fort Lee, N. J.
EHLERS, AUGUST	Los Angeles.
HOUGHTON, SHERMAN O. (Sergt.)	San Jose.
Ex-Mayor of San Jose, Ex-Recorder of Santa Clara Co. Ex-Member of Congress.	
HILL, THOMAS J.	San Francisco.
MacDONOUGH, JOSEPH	San Francisco.
Capt. in General Meagher's Brigade, late war.	
*MYERS, RUSSELL	New York City.
Major 3nd Regt. N. Y. Vols., late war.	
MUNSON, LEONARD A.	Two Rocks, Sonoma Co.
NOYES, MICHAEL S.	Eureka, Nevada.
O'SULLIVAN, JAMES	San Francisco.
Ex-Editor "Herald"—Sonoma, Toulumne Co.	
POST, FREDERICK L.	San Francisco.
Clerk S. F. Post Office, past 20 years.	
*PARVIN, JOHN B.	Monticello, Minn.
*PERRY, MOSES W.	Tucson, Arizona.
*ROGERS, WILLIAM H.	Brooklyn, N. Y.
*SCOLLAN, JOHN	Santa Barbara.
*SCHOONMAKER, JACOB J.	Vineland, N. J.
*SAUNDERS, THEODORE R.	New York City.
*THOMPSON, JAMES	Brooklyn, N. Y.
*THOMAS, JOHN W.	San Jose.
*WOOLEY, WILLIAM	Camp Seco, Calaveras, Co.
*WILLIAMS, WILLIAM H.	Nyack, N. Y.

Supposed to be Living.

TAIT, JAMES A.	Was at Santa Cruz, Cal., 1874.
FLOOD, JOHN	" " San Francisco, "
WILLARD, ISAAC	" in Mendocino Co., "
WELLER, EDWARD H.	" at San Francisco, "

Whereabouts Unknown.

Lieut. GEORGE F. PENROSE
Lieut. CHARLES B. YOUNG
ALBERGER, JOHN
BECKER, JOHN
BONCHALTZ, THEODORE
BURKE, JAMES
CHIPMAN, WALTER (Sergt.)
DOLLMAN, FREDERICK
FOSTER, WM. S.
FENLEY, DANIEL
HOFFMAN, GEORGE W.
HATHAWAY, JAMES M.
IRWIN, EDWARD (Sergt.)
HAMILTON, JAMES
LEWIS, JOSEPH B. (Mus.)
MORSE, HENRY
MURRAY, EDWARD
MORTON, FREEMAN
PEASLEY, NESMITH H.
PENNY, MOSES H.
RYAN, P. H. W.
SKINNER, JOHN
SUTPHEN, WILLIAM
SCHOONMAKER, M. C. (Corpl.)
SEIDER, GEORGE F.
THURSBY, LEWIS P. (Corpl.)
TAIT, WILLIAM G.
TIPSON, WILLIAM H.
WILSON, JAMES
WALSH, JAMES
WETTERMARK, CHARLES P.
WEIRGEN, CHRISTIAN

Deceased.

Lieut. GEORGE F. LEMON, .. { From wounds received in battle of Crampton Gap, Sept. 14, 1862.
City Assessor of S. F. in '51. Lieut.-Col. 32d Regt. N. Y. Vols. at date of death.

BROHAN, JOHN .. .. At Stockton, ———— 1850.
CURREN, EDWARD .. .. At ———— Cal. ———— 1860.
CARR, STEPHEN At Taylor's Ferry, Stanislaus River, Sept. — 1849.
DARREN, HENRY E. .. Drowned in Sacramento River, Nov. 9, 1849.
DIXON, JAMES F. .. .. Drowned in Gold Lake, January 30, 1880.
HEYLAND, JOHN .. .. .. At Stockton, Nov. 27, 1852.
HART, HENRY L. .. At La Paz, L. C., Aug. 20, 1848.
LUSKEY, JOSEPH .. .. .. Date and place unknown.
McDONOUGH, NICHOLAS .. Accidently killed at La Paz, L. C.
MURRAY, WALTER .. .. At San Luis Obispo, October 6, 1875
Ex-Member of the Cal. Legislature, and was the District Judge of First Judicial District at date of death.
McGILL, PATRICK .. .. Date and place unknown.
POWELLS, WILLIAM E. .. .. At Montery, Nov., 1848.
SWORDS, ALLEN J. .. La Paz, L. C., August 18, 1848.
THOMPSON, PETER .. .. Los Angeles, July 31, 1879.
TALMADGE, ABIJAH D. Killed by Mokelumne Indians, Dec. 1848.
VELSOR, STEPHEN .. .. .. Date and place unknown.
WHITLOCK, MERVIN R. .. Drowned in San Joaquin River, 1849.
WHITLOCK, JACOB H. .. San Francisco, ———, 1849.
HUXLEY, J. MEAD .. .. .. Date and place unknown.
Officer in the Army during the late War, rank unknown.

TRANSFERRED FROM CO. A.

√ ADAMS, JAMES H. .. .. To Co. G.
√ GRAHAM, GEORGE .. .. " F.
√ MERRILL, JOHN H. .. .. .. " K.
√ SULLIVAN, CORNELIUS .. " I.

Co. "B."

This Company was recruited by James M. Turner, at Harmony Hall, No. 17 Centre Street, New York. On the morning of the 1st of August the men assembled at this place and proceeded to the foot of Whitehall Street, *en route* to Governor's Island. When the regiment embarked in September for California, this Company was assigned to the ship "Thomas H. Perkins," in which ship they were conveyed to California, arriving at San Francisco on the 6th of March, 1847. After the arrival of the Company in California, its history is coincident with that of Company "A," given on another page.

Upon the departure of Captain Turner for New York, from Rio de Janeiro, the command devolved upon Lieutenant Henry C. Matsell, which he retained until the discharge of the Company at Monterey, on the 24th of October, 1848.

While the Company was stationed at La Paz, Lieutenant Thomas E. Ketchum (who came out in command of the recruits on the "Sweden"), reported for duty, and a part of the recruits by the "Isabella" were assigned to this Company to fill up its ranks. Lieutenant Ketchum and the recruits arrived at La Paz on the 15th of March, 1848, by the ship "Isabella."

Co. "B."

Survivors, April 15th, 1882.

*Lieut. THOMAS E. KETCHUM .. Stockton.
  Captain in the 3d Regiment California Volunteers, late war, now Brig.-General National Guard, State of California.
AMES, JOSIAH P. .. .. Half Moon Bay, San Mateo Co.
  Ex-Member of Californian Legislature, now Warder of the Cal. State Prison.
BADER, CHRISTOPHER .. Cherokee Flat, Butte Co.
*CATTS, SAMUEL A. .. Stockton.
CUNNINGHAM, ALEXANDER S. Fresno County.
DRYER, JOHN .. .. .. Santa Cruz, Cal.
*FARLEY, GEORGE .. The Dalles, Oregon.
FARLEY, THOMAS P Portland, Oregon.
GALLAGHER, JOHN St. Helena, Cal.
GREEN, ALFRED A. .. .. San Francisco.
  Ex-Member California Legislature, now Attorney-at-Law at S. F.
*HEINRICH, CHARLES .. .. Sacramento.
  Merchant past 25 years at Sacramento.
*HORNDELL, JOSEPH .. .. St. Louis, Mo.
LYNCH, PATRICK San Francisco.

*MOORE, ANDREW J. .. .. Philadelphia, Pa.
    *Member of the 72nd Regiment, Penn. Vols., late war.
OSTWALDT, AUGUST .. .. Sacramento.
*PEARSALL, SAMUEL W. ..   Mokelumne Hill.
*THURSTON, CHARLES II. .. ..   .. Marysville.
*McPHERSON, CHARLES J. (Mus.)   .;   New York City.
*NUTTMAN, JAMES E. .. ..   New York City.
    Ex-chief Engineer of Fire Department at Stockton,
    "   "   "   "   San Francisco.

Whereabouts Unknown.

Lieut. HENRY C. MATSELL
ADAMS, WASHINGTON
BOULANGEN, FRANCIS
BRADY, JOHN R.
BRIGHAM, E. R.
BALDWIN, JAMES H.
BLECKSMITH, LEOPOLD
CASEY, NEIL
COFFIN, WILLIAM
CARTER, GEORGE
CONNELLY, WILLIAM
FITCH, WORTHINGTON L.
GUILD, H. M. (Corpl.)
HELMSTADLER, JAMES
IHRIE, GEORGE
LUDLOFF, CHARLES
LAIDLAW, GEORGE
MASON, JOHN
McAULLY, ALEXANDER

McGUIRE, JOHN
MOUNICH, WILLIAM
PECK, CHAUNCEY L. (Corpl.)
PARSONS, ALONZO P
PAYSON, SAMUEL
RICHARDSON, CHARLES (Sergt.)
RITER, HENRY
RANDALL, CHARLES G.
RYAN, EDWARD
STARK, HENRY (Corpl.)
SMITH, LEWIS
SOMERS, FREDERICK
STONE, HEBER
ST. JOHN, AUGUSTUS A.
TURNER, LOAMMI
TINSON, JOHN
WEISS, WILLIAM (Corpl.)
WALL, RICHARD

Deceased.

Lieut. E. GOULD BUFFUM .. .. at Paris, France, Dec. 24, 1867.
    Journalist and author; Paris correspondent of the New York Herald at date of death.
CARNES, THOMAS .. .. .. Drowned in Stockton Slough, 1851.
CLARK, DANIEL P.   at San Diego, Sept. 24, 1879.
CONNELLY, MICHAEL   ..   Date and place unknown.
CLIFFORD, CORNELIUS .. .. at San Juan Mission, ——, 185—.
DENNISTON, JAMES G. (Sergt.) ..   at San Francisco, June 17, 1869.
    Ex-Member Californian Legislature.
DRENNER, JAMES .. .. .. Toulumne Co., August —, 1871.
FARLEY, JOHN G.   ..   ..   San Francisco, ——, 1849.
FARLEY JOHN (Son of John G.)   Portland, Oregon, ——, 187—.
HIPWOOD, THOMAS   killed in assault at San Antonio, L.C., March 16, 1848.
HARPER, THOMAS W.   .. Santa Barbara, June 28, 1856.

LAWSON, JOHN	Monterey, ——, 1849.
McGHEE, JOHN	San Francisco, Feb. 23, 1861.
MAXWELL, WILLIAM H.	New York City, Oct. 26, 1876.
MELVIN, JAMES W.	San Francisco, May 18, 1874.
MITCHELL, WILLIAM	Australia, N.S.W., ——.
MURPHY, JOHN	Stockton, ——, 185—.
OGDEN, BENJAMIN	at New York, 18—.
PECK, CHARLES L.	Date and place unknown.
PIERCE, CHARLES	Date and place unknown.
SCOTT, CHARLES G. (Sergt.)	Date and place unknown.
Ex-Treasurer of San Francisco County.	
STAYTON, JAMES (Sergt.)	near Calaveras River, Jan. 22, 1852.
SPATZ, CONRAD (Fifer)	Killed at La Paz, Nov. 16, 1847.
VAN BUSSUM, J. V.	Date and place unknown.
WHITEHOUSE, BENJAMIN	Stockton, ——, 185—.
WHITE, CHRISTOPHER S.	Date and place unknown.
WEEKS, ELBERT	Date and place unknown.

Transferred from Co. B.

BURGESS, EDWARD	to Co. G.
CAMPBELL, PETER	" H.
CLOUSSEN, HENRY	" G.
LANKOW, EDWARD	Regimental Band.
SMITH, JAMES	to Co. F.
STOLTZE, ADOLPH	" F.
TOYE, H. H. F.	" G.
WILT, JOHN (Sergt.)	" F.
VEAVIS, JOSE	" E.

Co. "C."

This Company was enlisted by John E. Brackett in the City of New York, and conveyed to California in the ship "Loo Choo," arriving at San Francisco on the 26th of March, 1847, and took post at Sonoma in the early part of April, at which place it remained until May, 1848, when the Company was ordered to San Jose near Cape San Lucas, Lower California, and had proceeded as far as Monterey, when the order was countermanded, and the command returned to Sonoma. On the 5th of August, 1848, the Company proceeded to the Presedio, San Francisco, exchanging posts with Company "H," stationed at that point. During the summer and Fall of 1847, a detatchment of 35 men from this Company was stationed at Fort Sacramento (Sutter's Fort) for five months.

An old resident of Sonoma, writing to the "Californian," at San Francisco—at that time the only newspaper published in California—under date of August 5th, 1848, among other subjects, pays the following compliment to this command:

"The military company under command of Captain J. E. Brackett are to-day exchanging posts with Company "H," under command of Captain Frisbie, both of the New York Volunteers. Company "C" has been stationed with us more than a year, and much praise is due its members, not only for the military and soldier-like manner in which they have acquited themselves as a corps, but for their gentlemanly and orderly deportment, individually and collectively. We regret to part with them, and cannot let them go without expressing a hope that, when peace shall have been declared, their regiment disbanded, and their country no longer needs their services, they may have fallen sufficiently in love with our healthy climate and our beautiful valley to come back and settle."

Co. "C."

Survivors, April 1st, 1882.

AURWELLER, JOHN	San Francisco.
*COX, ALEXANDER J.	Mendocino City, Cal.

Journalist; Founder of the Sonoma Bulletin in 1852.

DOTTER, WILLIAM C.	San Francisco.

Ex-Member Californian Legislature.

DOW, JOSEPH G.	Mendocino.
HUEFNER, WILLIAM	San Francisco.

Marshal, Society of California Pioneers, at S. F.

KAMP, HUROLD	Sonoma.
NORRIS, DAVID (Corpl.)	Centreville, Alameda Co.
RUSS, ADOLPH G.	San Francisco.
STORY, GEORGE	on Russian River, near Healdsburg.
WASHBURN, LYSANDER E.	San Francisco.

Captain, 3d Regiment, Cal. Vols., late war.

Supposed to be Living.

Lieut. THERON R., PER LEE .. .. was in New York City in 1880.
AMES, THADDEUS M. was M.D. at Indian Reservation, Men. Co., in 1860.
JONES, WILLIAM .. .. .. was in Sonoma Co. in 1874.

Whereabouts Unknown.

BARRET, FRANCIS H.
BERTRAND, EMILE
BALLARD, JOHN
CROSBY, EDMUND P. (Sergt.)
CAMERON, JOHN
    Ex-Mayor of Sonoma.
CONRAD, HENRY
DELEHAYE, CHARLES
DE ST. QUINTAIN, JOSEPH
DONEGAN, JOHN
DOUGHERTY, JAMES
ELB, FREDERICK
GLOSS, JOHN
HIGGINS, SILAS G.
HOW, OLIVER H.
JOHNSON, WILLIAM (Sergt.)
KIESLER, LAFAYETTE
KLENGEL, FRANCIS
KENTZBURY, ADOLPHUS

KROHN, JOHN M.
KAPPIS, GEORGE
LYNCH, FERDINAND
MINARD, THOMAS A.
MILLER, FRANCIS
NAGLE, FERDINAND
PETERSON, FREDERICK
PRENTICE, CHARLES
RUB, GEORGE
ROEDER, LOUIS
SCOTT, WILLIAM
SMITH, GERARD D.
STRANGE, JOHN
TIMEANS, CHARLES (Mus.)
WEAVER, WILLIAM J.
WELDER, ANTHONY
WILLHART, LOUIS
ZETSCHSKY, CHARLES

Deceased.

Capt. JOHN E. BRACKETT .. .. .. Date and place unknown.
  Ex-Member Californian Legislature, 1850; Ex-Major-Genl. Cal. State Militia.
Lieut. THOMAS J. ROACH, { Drowned near Young's Ferry, on Klamath River, Nov. 11, 1852.
  Ex-Deputy Collector Port of San Francisco; County Judge elect of Klamath Co. at time of death.
Lieut. CHARLES C. ANDERSON   at San Francisco, Sept. 13, 1847.
CUSHING, BELA (Corpl.) .. .. Sonoma, Jan. 13, 1848.
CONWAY, JOHN P. .. .. .. San Francisco, ——, 18—.
FOSTER, BENJAMIN F.   Portsmouth, N.H., July 21, 1865.
GREEN, WILLIAM G. ..   .. San Rafael, Aug. 1, 1871.
KONIG, WILLIAM   Drowned in Sacramento River, June 11, 1847.
KINNS, ALEXANDER   Found dead near Sonoma, Dec. 19, 1847.
LAYDEN, WILLIAM   .. .. Date and place unknown.
McCARTY, DAVID C. .. .. San Francisco, Sept. 9, 1868.
McCARTY, EDWARD   Santa Barbara, April 5, 1852.
RAND, JOSHUA .. .. Date and place unknown.
RICHARDSON, ARTEMUS. .. Somona, Cal., July 12, 1854.
RUMSCHOTTEL, RICHARD **Drowned at Stockton, July** 10, 1874.
RUSS, J. C. CHRISTIAN .. .. .. San Francisco, June 4, 1857.
  First Jeweler and Watchmaker established at S. F.

Deceased en *Voyage.*

Lieut. WILLIAM R. TREMMELS ..   off Cape Horn, ——, 1846.

Transferred from Co. C.

v	Lieut. GEORGE D. BREWERTON ..	to Co. K.
v	ROBINSON, GEORGE (Sergt.) ..	" G.
v	MORRISON, RODERICK M...	" K.
/	WEHLER, EDWARD ..	to Regimental Band.
v	WADDELL, ARCHIBALD	.. .. to Co. E.
v	YOUNG, CHARLES D. ..	.. to Regimental Band.

Co. "D."

This Company was enlisted at La Fayette Hall, Broadway, opposite Nibblo's Garden, New York City, in the summer of 1846. Many of its members came from Philadelphia, Captain Henry M. Naglee himself being a Pennsylvanian. Upon the embarkation of the regiment for California, the Company was assigned to the ship "Susan Drew," which reached San Francisco March 19th, 1847. On the 1st of April the Company embarked on board the U. S. Storeship "Lexington," and on the 3d sailed for Monterey, reaching that port on the 4th. While stationed at Monterey, portions of the Company were mounted and sent upon several expeditions in quest of Indian horse-thieves in the San Joaquin Valley and the Sierra Nevada Mountains. These men traveled many days and encamped at nights upon the same ground in which were afterwards found such rich gold deposits. On the 5th of March, 1848, the Company sailed in the ship "Isabella" for La Paz, Lower California, arriving there on the 22d of the same month. At La Paz the Company was filled up to 100 men, from recruits which had recently arrived by the ships "Isabella" and "Sweden." One week after their arrival at La Paz, Lieut.-Col. Burton, with Companies A, B and D, made a march into the interior, had an engagement with the Mexican Forces at Todas Santos, completely dispersing the enemy and driving them from the peninsula. After an absence of two weeks the command returned to La Paz, and, on the 15th of April, Co. D embarked on board the U. S. Storeship "Southampton" for San Jose del Cabo, and within three days relieved the Naval Forces stationed at that town, which they continued to garrison until the 6th of Sept., 1848, upon which date the Company hauled down the stars and stripes and evacuated Mexican soil. The Company embarked on the U. S. Ship of the Line "Ohio," which conveyed them to Monterey, Upper California, where they were discharged. *This Company was without doubt the last command of American troops to leave the soil of Mexico after the close of the Mexican War.*

Co. "D."

Survivors, April 15th, 1882.

Capt. HENRY M. NAGLEE	San Jose.
Brig.-General of Vols. late war.	
*CHANDLER, JOHN A.	Boston, Mass.
*CORGAN, GEORGE A.	Chicago, Ill.
Vice-Pres. Ass'n. Vets. of the Mex. War, Chicago.	
*CLARK, FRANCIS D.	New York City.
Justice of the Peace San Joaquin County 1852, 3 and 4: Major and Military Secretary, Department of North Carolina, under Hon. Edward Stanly, late war.	
*DEAN, GEORGE C.	Visalia.
GRAY, JAMES A.	Salinas City.
Ex-Member of California Legislature.	
*HARRON, JAMES M.	Sentinel, Fresno Co.
HAVEY, JOHN	West Point, Calaveras Co.
*JOHNSON, WILLIAM S.	Salinas City.
Ex-County Recorder, Ex-County Clerk and Ex-County Treasurer of Monterey Co.; now cashier Salinas City Bank.	
*LIPP, CARL	Vallejo.
MOORE, ANDREW	Gilroy.
MYERS, GEORGE	Mount Eden, Alameda Co.
*NORRIS, JACOB W.	Newark, N. J.
Now Sergeant of Police, Newark, N. J.	
PHILLIPS, JOHN B.	San Francisco.
REAUSSEAU, CHARLES	San Francisco.
*ROBINSON, WILLIAM D.	Monterey.
*SIMS, JOSEPH	Sacramento.
TOMBS, GEORGE W.	Modesto.
Ex-Treasurer of Stanislaus Co.	
WOODSIDE, PRESTON K.	Tucson, Arizona.
Ex-Clerk Supreme Court, State of California.	
*WOLFE, JOHN	New York City.
YOUNG, ALPHIAS	San Francisco.

Supposed to be Living.

HILL, JOHN E.	was at Pendleton, Umatilla Co., Oregon, in 1878.
BUDD, CHARLES K.	Sonoma County in 1868.

Whereabouts Unknown.

ATKINSON, CHARLES A.	BOSTWICK, JAMES C.
AMES, EDWARD T.	BOCHON, PROCOPI
ATHERTON, GEORGE D.	CLAUSEN, WILLIAM (Mus.)
BUCKBEE, FLAVIUS (Corpl.)	CASTON, GEORGE R.
BARTELS, LEWIS	COHN, PHILIP
BOND, WILLIAM	DELICK, JOHN
BARGEMAN, AUGUSTUS	DARRAH, DECATUR

DOOLAN, JOHN
ELLIS, THOMAS W.
ENNIS, JOHN
FORBES, HECTOR M.
FERMOR, EDWARD
GRAY, ALONZO
HETHERINGTON, WILLIAM E.
HAYDEN, GEORGE W.
HEYDENRICH, WILLIAM
HARRINGTON, JOHN
HAAG, FREDERICK
HACKETT, PATRICK
HUGHES, JOHN
HAGEMAN, CHARLES K.
JENKINS, WILLIAM K.
JAMES, ALDEN W.
KUTCHBACK, CHARLES
KEAPNELL, FREDERICK
KENNEDY, EDWARD P.
LOCKWOOD, ISAAC
LEICK, CHARLES
MARKET, AUGUSTINE
McCARRAN, JOSEPH
MULHOLLAND, DOMINEC
McCLUSKY, PHILIP
MILLER, HENRY
McINTYRE, TERANCE
MAGER, ADAM

MUNROE, JOHN
MORIN, JOHN L.
MILLER, JOHN
MOFFITT, WILLIAM B.
NEWITT, SAMUEL
NEWMAN, JAMES
NEIMAN, HENDRICK
OGLE, CHARLES A.
PATTERSON, JOHN A.
POINEER, JACOB A.
ROBINSON, WILLIAM
RILEY, JAMES
ROBB, JAMES B.
SANFORD, SAMUEL
SEARLES, GEORGE
SCOTT, ANDREW
SINCLAIR, ARCHIBALD
SHOOTER, CHARLES
SCHRAELOR, GEORGE
SWEET, CHARLES C.
SOHNS, JOHN
TURNER, DAVID
VAN AUKEN, PHILANDER
WILSON, HENRY J. (Sergt.)
WILSON, JOHN
WALZ, GEORGE
WARRINGTON, JOHN

Deceased.

Lieut. GEORGE A. PENDLETON .. .. San Diego, March 3, 1871
County Clerk of San Diego Co. at date of death.
Lieut. HIRAM W. THEALL .. .. Hamilton, White Pine, Nevada.
Lieut. JOSEPH C. MOREHEAD .. . Date and place unknown
ASHTON, GEORGE HENRY { Killed by Indians in the San Joaquin Valley, 1847
ANDERSON, FRANCIS P. .. San Francisco, Oct. 5, 1881.
BOWERS, JAMES H. .. .. Stockton, Cal., ——, 185—.
CLAPP, CHARLES D. .. Sydney, N. S. W., ——, 185—.
CLARK, FRANCIS C. .. .. Camp on Merced River, 1853.
EDWARDS, JOHN S. Drowned in San Joaquin River, April 4, 1854.
FRIUND, HENRY J. .. .. .. Date and place unknown.
HART, JOHN .. .. Date and place unknown.
HARLEY, HENRY .. near Sacramento, ——, 187—.
HILTON, BENJAMIN .. Monterey, Sept. 23, 1847.
IVEN, ALFRED .. Acapulco, Mexico, ——, 1851.
JUDSON, HENRY .. Mokelumne Hill, ——, 1849.

KEHOE, JOSEPH H. .. .. Monterey, Oct. 18, 1848.
LYONS, AARON (Sergt.) .. .. Monterey, Oct. 2, 1865.
Ex-Sheriff of Monterey Co.
LASKEY, ALEXANDER B. .. .. Killed by Indians, ———, 1848.
McKEE, JAMES M. .. .. Monterey, Dec. 21, 1847.
MOORE, JOHN W. .. .. Killed by Indians, Mariposa, 1851.
MORAN, JOHN H. . .. San Francisco, Feb. 17, 1871.
McCLASKY, WILLIAM J .. .. San Francisco, Oct. 24, 1866.
MOUSER, JOHN Drowned in San Joaquin River, June 3, 1847.
PURDY, SAMUEL L. .. .. San Jose, L. C., June 11, 1848.
ROACH, WILLIAM (Sergt.) .. .. Monterey Co., Sept. 3, 1866.
Ex-Sheriff of Monterey Co.
RYAN, WILLIAM REDMOND .. .. .. New Orleans, ———, 1852.
Author of "Personal Recollections in Upper and Lower California," published in London, 1852.
SIREY, JAMES .. .. .. Date and place unknown.
SUCKET, LEON .. .. San Francisco, Aug. 29, 1871.
TILEE, DANIEL E. .. .. New York, ———, 187—.
WHEELER, WILLIAM H. H. .. San Jose, L. C., Aug. 12, 1848.

Transferred from Co. D.

McDONALD, ALEXANDER C. .. Promoted to Sergeant-Major.
GRAY, ALONZO .. .. to Co. E.
GUIBAL, EUGENE .. .. " I.
KEMPT, GEORGE W. .. " I.
MITCHELL, WILLIAM " B.
RUSSELL, WILLIAM .. " G.
MASSE, ANTONIO .. to Regimental Band.

Co. "E."

This Company was recruited by Nelson Taylor, Thomas H. Ferris and William E. Cutrell, who were upon its organization elected, and subsequently commissioned, respectively, its captain and first and second lieutenants. Ferris, before the regiment left New York, resigned, and Edward Williams was commissioned in his stead. Thomas L. Vermule was also commissioned an additional second lieutenant.

The men who formed this Company were principally from the East side of New York City, while many came from the Ninth Ward on the West side, headed by Sergeants Van Riper and O'Neil.

On the 1st of July, 1846, recruiting for the Company commenced at the old Seventh Ward Democratic Head-quarters, then kept by Daniel Hughes in Madison Street. Another office was also opened for a few days at the corner of Fulton and Nassau Streets. On the 1st day of August the Company was marched to the regimental rendezvous on Governor's Island, in New York Harbor, and a few days subsequently were mustered into the service by Colonel Bankhead.

Upon the embarkation of the regiment in September it was found necessary to divide one of the Companies into three sections, there being ten companies in the regiment and only three transports, the honor therefore of being represented on each of the ships fell to this Company. Captain Taylor was lying sick at his home at the time of the embarkation of the regiment; he had, however, arranged to be carried on board the ship "Thomas H. Perkins," but owing to the negligence of the officer having the matter in charge, he failed to be notified, and the fleet sailed, leaving him in New York. Captain Taylor was subsequently assigned to the command of about fifty officers and privates who had been left behind, and sailed for California in the transport "Brutus," arriving at San Francisco one month later than the regiment.

This Company also embarked on board the U. S. Storeship "Lexington," and arrived at Monterey, April 4th, 1847, at which place they were stationed until the 5th of May, when they again sailed in the "Lexington" for San Pedro, and reached Los Angeles on the 9th, which post was made the Head-quarters of the regiment. The Company remained at Los Angeles until the 18th of September, 1848, when it was mustered out of the service. The good health of the Company during its whole term of service was remarkable—not a member was lost by sickness and but two from injuries.

Colonel Stevenson compliments thus the soldiers of Cos. E and G. He says, "the two companies of Los Angeles were noted for their orderly and soldierly bearing, and for their prompt and faithful discharge of their military duties."

Co. "E."

Survivors, April. 15th, 1882.

*Capt. NELSON TAYLOR .. .. . South Norwalk, Conn.
Ex-Member California Legislature; President of the First Board of Trustees, State Insane Asylum, Stockton Cal.; Ex-Sheriff of San Joaquin Co.; Brig.-Genl. of Vols. late war.

Lieut. EDWARD WILLIAMS .. .. Oakland.
BOYERS, WILLIAM (Corpl.) .. ... San Francisco.
BULLOCK, EZEKIAL ... .. San Francisco.

BRIGGS, CASTOR .. San Francisco.
*BARTLETT, JOHN A. .. .. Cambridgeport, Mass.
*CANFIELD, GEORGE W. Philadelphia, Pa.
GRAFF, GEORGE J. .. San Francisco.
*JOHNSON, ISAAC C. .. .. .. Astoria, Oregon.
*LEONARD, GEORGE W. M. New York City.
*O'NEIL, JOHN M. (Sergt.) .. .. San Francisco.
    Major 2nd Cal. Cavalry late war; now Officer of the Customs, S. F.
*WELSH, JOHN H. .. .. New York City.
WOHLGEMOUTH, HENRY J. .. .. San Francisco.

Supposed to be Living.

LOWERY, ANTHONY W. .. was at San Francisco in 1878.
SNYDER, ELIJAH .. .. Trenton, N. J., in 1875.
SOUERVOIT, ALEXANDER Los Angeles in 1877.

Whereabouts Unknown.

ACKLEY, HENRY (Corpl.)
BURTON, JAMES C. (Mus.)
BLAIR, CHARLES D.
BAXTER, WILLIAM
BRUSLE, WASHINGTON
BROWN, CHARLES
BOGART, HENRY
BUCKLE, ROBERT
BALL, FRANKLIN
BARRY, BENJAMIM
BALDWIN, TIMOTHY
CALDER, LAWSON M. (Corpl,)
CAMPBELL, JAMES T.
CLARK, GEORGE
CHICHESTER, HENRY T.
DEAS, JAMES
DRIEHER, JACOB
FORBES, ELI B.
FOLEY, ALFRED
GOLDEN, EDWARD
HAMLEN, MORTIMER J.
HENRY, JAMES
HUTCHEON, WALTER
HEARN, THOMAS
HITCHCOCK, JOHN C.
HUMPHREY, BENJAMIN F.
HALL, JOHN
JAMIESON, GEORGE WILLIAM
KINTRING, CHARLES M.
KIERNAN, JOHN B.
KENNERSLY, A. J.
LAMBERT, JOHN A.
LEGARE, BURNETT

LINTON, JAMES
McPHERSON, GEORGE (Mus.)
MORTON, HENRY S. (Sergt.)
McMANUS, JAMES (Sergt.)
McGILL, JAMES
MITCHELL, WILLIAM H.
MILLIKEN, JOHN
MORRISON, LUDLAM *
MOORE, JOHN H.
MURPHY, THOMAS
McGRANAGHAN, WILLIAM G.
OWENS, ALEXANDER
OLPSTAY, JACOB
PERKINS, CHARLES
PARKER, EDWARD
PLUNKETT, JAMES
PLUMMER, WILLIAM
RICHARDS, JAMES
RAMSEY, JOHN W.
ROBERTS, SAMUEL
SMITH, JOHN M.
SWARTS, JOHN S.
SNITTER, LEWIS
STACK, GARRETT
VAN RIPER, ABRAHAM (Sergt.)
VORHEES, JOHN
VINSON, WILLIAM
WINNIE, WILLIAM
WHITE, MOSES
WYLIE, JOHN
WADDELL, ARCHIBALD
WEIFENBACK, PHILIP
YEAMANS, EDWARD

Deceased.

Lieut. WILLIAM E. CUTRELL ..   San Francisco, May 28, 1868.
Lieut. THOMAS L. VERMULE .. .. .. San Jose, ——, 18—.
   Member of the State Constitutional Convention at Monterey in 1849; Ex-Member of the California Legislature.
BRUSLE, JACKSON   Contra Costa Co., Feb. 14, 1854.
BLAIR, NICHOLAS ..   Los Angeles, Sept. 26, 1855.
BARTLETT, CHARLES H. .. .. San Francisco, May 15, 1881.
BROCKEE, JOSEPH .. Drowned in Stanislaus River, March, 1849.
DEY, NATHAN B.   .. .. Los Angeles, July 7, 1848.
EARLE, PETER .. .. Sacramento, Jan. 12, 1871.
FORD, PATRICK .. .. Killed by Rogue River Indians, ——, 1866.
LEGARE, WILLIAM H. .. .. Los Angeles, Dec. 9, 1847.
MARK, LOUIS .. .. Date and place unknown.
MEEHAN, THOMAS { Killed by Steamboat Explosion on the San Joaquin River, Oct. 19, 1853.
MEEHAN, DENNIS .. .. .. Killed at Stockton, Fall of 1849.
PARKER, LEWIS .. ..Date and place unknown.
TAYLOR, JOHN .. .. .. New York, April 28, 1879.
THAFFER, ANDREW   San Francisco, May 3, 1879.
VAN PELT, JACOB   San Francisco, Nov. 15, 1849.

Transferred from Co. E.

GILLINGHAM, HENRY ..   to Co. I.
McKAY, JOHN H.   .. .. " K.
WHALEN, JOHN .. . to Regimental Band.

Co. "F."

At the date of the embarkation of the regiment at New York, this Company was assigned to the ship "Thomas H. Perkins," and reached San Francisco on the 6th of March, 1847. On the 8th of the following month the Company reached Santa Barbara (see Co. A), at which place it did garrison duty until their discharge from the service on the 8th of September, 1848.

Co. "F."

Survivors, April 15th, 1882.

*Capt. FRANCIS J. LIPPITT ..   Washington, D.C.
   Member of the State Constitutional Convention at Monterey, 1849; elected Colonel 1st Reg't California Volunteers, June 27, 1861.
*Lieut. HENRY STORROW CARNES   .. San Buenaventura.
   Ex-District Judge 2d Jud. District, California; Ex-Member Legislature, Cal.; Postmaster at Santa Barbara, 1870 to 1874.
*ENGELBERG, AUGUST E. .. .. .. San Francisco.
FLYING, ANDREW   .. Santa Barbara.

*LYNCH, JAMES	Jolon, Monterey Co.
MILLHAUSE, GUSTAVE	Santa Barbara.
RUSS, AUGUST	San Francisco.
*RUSS, CHARLES C. E.	San Francisco.
SCHLOTTHOUER, CARL	Rough and Ready.
SESSER, PETER	San Francisco.
*WHITAKER, AMISON	Sacramento.

Supposed to be Living.

LOPEZ, THEODORE	was at Tuolumne Co. in 1874.
MILFORD, EDMUND N.	Bodie, Mono Co., in 1880.
WILLIS, OTTIS W.	San Andreas in 1874.

Whereabouts Unknown.

Lieut. WILLIAM H. WEIRICK	McMILLAN, CHARLES
CARPENTER, CHARLES R.	McCRACKEN, WILLIAM R.
COOPER, JAMES F.	McLEOD, FRANCIS J
COE, JOHN J.	MASON, ALFRED
DOULEVY, JAMES	POWER, EDWARD (Corpl.)
EVANS, RANDOLPH	PULIS, JOHN C. (Sergt.)
FLEETWOOD, ROBERT	POWER, JOHN A.
FIELD, JOHN	RIGBY, GEORGE F. (Corpl.)
FIELD DANIEL	SMITH, THEODORE
FULLER, WILLIAM M.	SARGENT, JAMES K.
GALUSHA, ELON A.	SHURTS, WATSON
GRAHAM, GEORGE	SMITH, JAMES G.
HUGHES, WILLIAM (Corpl.)	SMITH, HENRY J.
JORDAN, PHILIP	STEPHENS, PETER
KING, WILLIAM	STOLZE, ADOLPHUS
KONTZ, JOHN G.	TROUTMAN, JAMES B.
LEE, JOHN C.	TROUTMAN, JOHN (Drummer)
LEFORT, GEORGE	VIDAL, JOHN A.
MULVEY, JAMES (Sergt.)	WINDMEYER, RICHARD
McSPADDEN, JAMES	

Deceased.

Lieut. JOHN M. HUDDART	at Sandwich Islands, ——, 185—.
BATHGATE, GEORGE	Date and place unknown.
DELANEY, RICHARD E.	at San Francisco, Sept. 20, 1876.
GANNON, THOMAS	at Santa Barbara, Dec. 30, 1855.
GORMLY, MARTIN F.	Killed by Steam Explosion, April 15, 1854.
HEFFERNAN, CHARLES	at San Francisco, ——, 18—.
HASKELL, JOHN W.	at Santa Barbara, April 13, 1878.
LEE, CORNELIUS R. V.	at Santa Barbara, Jan. 11, 1863.
LEWIS, JOHN	at Santa Barbara, April 27, 1848.
OAKLEY, ROBERT	at Santa Barbara, Jan. 1, 1848.

ROANE, ARCHIBALD	at Georgetown, D. C., Sept. 3, 1879.
STOCKTON, WILLIAM B.	Date and place unknown.
STOTHERS, JOHN E.	Oakland, ——, 187—.
SCHRIVES, DANIEL B.	Date and place unknown.
TINDALL, WILLIAM	at San Francisco, ——, 18—.
WILT, JOHN	Date and place unknown.
QUEEN, JAMES (Sergt.)	.. at Napa, Dec. 7, 1879.
WEBSTER, JOHN H. ..	.. at Stockton, June 10, 1881.
MAXFELD, WILLIAM C. .	Date and place unknown.

Transferred from Co. F.

Lieut. JEREMIAH SHERWOOD	.. .. to Co. G.
ECHER, JOHN	.. to Regimental Band.
HIPWOOD, THOMAS (Sergt.)	to Co. B.
LOW, JAMES C.	Promoted to Quarter-Master Sergeant.

Co. "G."

This Company was organized under the direction of Matthew R. Stevenson, a son of the Colonel, to which he was subsequently elected Captain, and made the voyage to San Francisco in the ship "Thomas H. Perkins." On the 3d of April in company with "D," "E" and "I" sailed from Monterey in the U. S. Storeship "Lexington." In May the Company with Co. "E" re-embarked in the "Lexington" for San Pedro, taking post at Los Angeles (Head-quarters of the regiment), where the Company remained until discharged from the service on the 18th of September, 1848.

Co. "G."

Survivors, April 15th, 1882.

*Lieut. JOHN McH. HOLLINGSWORTH	Georgetown, D. C.
Member of State Constitutional Convention at Monterey in 1849.	
*Lieut. JEREMIAH SHERWOOD	New York City.
Ex-Member of N. Y. Legislature.	
*ADAMS, JAMES H.	San Francisco.
JANTZEN, FREDERIC	San Francisco.
KLEINSHOOTH, JOHN	.. .. Germany.
*NISBITT, THOMAS ..	Scott River, Siskiyou Co.
SHIRLAND, E. D.	.. Auburn, Placer Co.
Capt. of Vol's, late war; Ex-County Clerk and Recorder of Sacramento Co.	
SCHUMAKER, JOHN	.. Los Angeles.

SHROTER, CHARLES	.. San Francisco.
PFIESTER, ADOLPH	.. San Jose.
Ex-Mayor of San Jose, now capitalist and merchant.	
TIEROFF, AUGUSTUS	. San Francisco.
WELLS, THOMAS JEFFERSON	New York City.
*WILSON, ROBERT	Vallejo.

Supposed to be Living.

CHAQUETH, HERMAN	was at San Francisco in 1874.
COYAN, FREDERICK	was at Vallejo in 1874.
FALKNER, JAMES Y. (Corpl.)	was in Oregon in 1878.
FRESCHE, FRANCIS	was at San Francisco in 1874.
STEVENS, JOHN H.	was at Stockton in 1874.

Whereabouts Unknown.

BOINGER, FREDERIC	LYNCH, JOSEPH P. (Corpl.)
BENNETT, TITUS	LINDER, FRANCIS
BURGEMAN, EMILE	MALCOLM, ALEXANDER B.
CONNELL, JOHN (Sergt.)	MONTRIEL, HERMAN
CAULTFIELD, PATRICK	MILLER, EDWARD
CAULTFIELD, DAVID	MILLER, VALENTINE
CLARK, JOHN	MILLER, CHARLES
CUMMINGS, JAMES	MARK, JOSEPH
COLGAN, JAMES A.	McDONALD, WILLIAM
COPENGER, CHARLES	MYERS, **JOHN**
CORNING, OTTO	**NORTHMAN, CHARLES**
CUVELLIER, EMIL	**OSBORNE, CHARLES**
COMSTOCK, CORTEY	PFEIFFER, **MAX WILLIAM**
DUNNE, JOHN	PHILLIPS, **JAMES**
DOOLEY, THOMAS	RUTH, **JOHN**
DIDDLESON, AUGUSTUS	RUSSELL, **WILLIAM**
EDMONSON, ALFRED	ROSE, JOHN M.
EUTH, JOHN	REISH, JACOB
EATON, GEORGE	ROWAN, **JAMES**
FARR, PHILIP	ROBINSON, GEORGE (Sergt.)
FITZSIMMONS, JAMES	SWAB, EMANUEL
GOODWILL, JAMES T.	SHISLYLIND, GUSTAFF (Mus.)
HANTON, MATTHEW O.	SHULTZE, FREDERIC
JACKSON, GEORGE (Sergt.)	SILTZER, HENRY
JACKSON, GEORGE (2nd)	SCHIMER, EARNEST
JOHNSON, FREDERICK (Corpl.)	SAXTON, CHARLES
JONES, JOHN	TAYLOR, WALTER (Sergt.)
KAUFMAN, JULIUS	TINKERMANN, MICHAEL
KENNEDY, WILLIAM A.	UPSON, TRUEMAN
KURTZ, LEWIS	VALLELY, **JOHN**
LAWRENCE, HENRY (Mus.)	WARREN, **JAMES**
LIPPER, AUGUSTUS	WELLS, WILLIAM
LELONG, MARTIN	WHEELER, WILLIAM M.
LEWIS, HENRY	WEBSTER, CHARLES A. **(1st)**

42

Deceased.

Capt. MATTHEW R. STEVENSON ..	at Sackett Harbor, Jan. 2, 1863.
ANDREWS, ALLEN	at Los Angeles, Dec. 9, 1847.
BOSQUE, THOMAS	.. at Los Angeles, Aug. 7, 1847.
BULTICE, VINCENT ..	.. Date and place unknown.
GRINNELL, CHARLES C. ..	Date and place unknown.
HART, JEROME	.. at Shasta, Feb. 4, 1852.
HOPPER, WILLIAM	.. .. at Los Angeles, July 12, 1847.
HAMMER, ROBERT	at Spanish Bar, American River, 1849.
MEHAN, JAMES (Sergt.)	.. Killed at Los Angeles, ——, 185—.
OSBOURN, WILLIAM B.	.. at Los Angeles, July 31, 1867.
SULLIVAN, JOHN	at San Luis Rey, Aug. 25, 1848.
TRAVERS, WILLIAM B. (Sergt.)	at Los Angeles, Dec. 10, 1847
THORNER, FRANCOIS ..	.. at Los Angeles, July 31, 1848.
TOYE, H. F. H. ..	.. Date and place unknown
TITTLE, AUGUSTUS	.. at San Francisco, Feb. 1, 1868.
UHRBROOK, HENRY	.. at Santa Clara, ——, 1875.
VANDERBECK, JAMES	at San Francisco, Sept. 23, 1849.
WEST, THOMAS J	.. Date and place unknown.
WEBSTER, CHARLES A. (2nd) ..	.. at Los Angeles, Aug. 17, 1847.
WORT, GEORGE	at San Francisco, April 5, 1847.

Transferred from Co. G.

Lieut. WILLIAM H. WEIRICK	to Co. F.
Lieut. WILLIAM H. SMITH ..	" I
BROWN, PHILIP	" H
CARR, STEPHEN	" A.
COOPER, SAMUEL ..	" F.
DUNITCH, ERNEST F. ..	to Regimental Band
FETSCHOROR, CHRISTIAN	" "
GRAMBIS, FREDERICK	" "
HASKELL, JOHN W	.. to Co. F.
HARRIS, STEPHEN	Promoted to Qr.-Mr. Sergeant.
HAUFF, ERNEST	to Regimental Band.
KRAUSS, CHARLES	" "
KLEINBROTH, JOHN ..	" "
LANKOW, EDWARD ..	to Co. B.
MURRAY, JOHN FRANCIS ..	" H.
POWERS, EDWARD ..	" F.
POWERS, JOHN	" F.
RICHARDSON, ARTEMUS W. ..	" C.
ROANE, ARCHIBALD ..	" F.
STALL, ALFRED ..	" I.
TITTLE, GOODLIP .. ;.	" I.
TESHNER, CHRISTIAN	to Regimental Band.

Co. "H."

This Company was recruited at Albany, N. Y., by John B. Frisbie and Edward Gilbert, who upon its organization were elected respectively its captain and first lieutenant. On the evening of the 31st of July, 1846, the Company left Albany by steamboat, reaching New York early the following morning. The Company was escorted from the steamboat to the foot of Whitehall Street by Captain Cooke's Company of Artillery and the Albany Washington Riflemen; the latter Company fired a salute upon the embarkation of the Company at the Battery for Governor's Island, the rendezvous of the regiment.

Upon the embarkation of the regiment this Company was assigned to the ship "Susan Drew," and arrived at San Francisco on the 19th of March 1847, and was stationed at the Presedio until the 5th of Aug., 1848, when it exchanged post with "C" at Sonoma. A few weeks later the Company returned to San Francisco, and was mustered out of the service on the 25th of August, 1848.

Co. "H."

Survivors April 15th, 1882.

*Capt. JOHN B. FRISBIE .. .. City of Mexico.
Nominated for Lieut. Gov. with Gen. John A. Sutter for Governor at the first election for State Officers in California.
*CORNWELL, GEORGE N. ... Napa.
Ex-Prefect of Sonoma District; Ex-Postmaster of Napa, (8 years); Ex-Member of the California Legislature, served several terms; 3 years Supervisor, and 6 years Under Sheriff, Sonoma Co.
EDMONSON, ——— .. .. .. San Francisco.
FRISBIE, ELEAZER (Sergt.) .. .. Vallejo.
*FOLSOM, WILLIAM H, ... New York City.
*GOLDWAITE, RICHARD M. .. .. .. Albany, N.Y.
GUTHRIE, WILLIAM .. Coulterville, Mariposa Co.
LAMPMAN, WILLIAM L. .. Republic of Mexico.
*LAPPEUS, JAMES H. .. .. Portland, Oregon.
Ex-City Marshal of Portland, Oregon; for the past twelve years has been Chief of Police, same city.
LEE, JAMES R. .. .. Vallejo.
*MERRILL, SQUIRE G. (Mus.) .. Washington, D. C.
REID, JOSEPH .. .. Napa.
*VAN VECHTEN, GEORGE .. New Brunswick, N. J
*YATES, JOHN D. .. .. Albany, N. Y.

Supposed to be Living.

BENJAMIN, FORDYCE I. .... was at Sonoma in 1874.
GROW, WILLIAM (Sergt.) .. .. was at Yreka in 1878.
    Ex-Sheriff of Siskiyou Co.; Ex-Postmaster at Yreka.
HUMPHREY, GEORGE L. .. .. .. was at Coulterville in 1874.

Whereabouts Unknown.

AGNEW, HUGH
BRAUN, PHILIP
COUTAN, GUSTAVUS J.
CARRIGAN, THOMAS
CAMPBELL, PETER
DAVIS, BENJAMIN B. (Corpl.)
GORDWELL, JAMES F.
GERRINGER, ANDREW
HUMPHREY, GEORGE L.
HARNES, HENRY
LATHROP, GEORGE W.
LAWSON, HENRY

LEGGETT, WILLIAM
LEDDY, MICHAEL
McCARTNEY, BARTHOLOMEW
MAPLE, JOHN
NORTON, MARTIN
NEWMAN, JOHN
RAMSEY, DAVID (Corpl.)
SHULTERS, JOHN
WISSELL, FREDERICK
WILLIE, HENRY
WIERZBICKIE, F. P.

Deceased.

Lieut. EDWARD GILBERT   at Oak Grove, near Sacramento, Aug. 2, 1852.
    Member of the State Constitutional Convention at Monterey in 1849; Ex-Member of Congress; Ex-Editor and Publisher of the "Alta California."

Lieut. JOHN S. DAY .... at Chicago, Ill., Oct. 14, 1851.
BEATTIE, BELDEN (Corpl.) .. at San Francisco, ——, 1849.
CRAFTS, ALBERT B. .... at San Francisco, May 10, 1849.
DAVIS, DAVID A. .. .. at San Jose, Dec. 18, 1848.
LANDERS, WILLIAM .... at Mission Dolores, S. F., 1850.
MURRAY, FRANCIS .. .. .. Date and place unknown.
MARTIN, WILLIAM H. .. Dry Creek, Stanislaus Co., June 23, 1874.
O'CONNELL, ANTHONY F... .. .. San Francisco, Jan. 22, 1866.
PURCELL, MATTHIAS .. .. San Francisco, ——, 1850.
SCHOOLCRAFT, HENRY A. (Sergt.) at Sea, near Acapulco, Mex., May 5, 1853.
    Ex-Collector, Port of Sacramento.
SHERMAN, HERAN V. S. .. .. Date and place unknown.
SLADE, WILLIAM D. .. Date and place unknown.
    Ex-City Marshal of Yreka.
SMITH, HENRY .... Drowned in Feather River, ——, 1849.
TIGHE, JOHN .. .. Date and place unknown.
VEEDER, PETER G. .. Date and place unknown.
WINNE, JAMES (Sergt.) .. .. Date and place unknown.

Transferred from Company D.

FULLER, WILLIAM M.	to Co. F.
HART, JEROME	" G.
HOHN, HENRY	to Regimental Band.
ROANE, JOHN	" "
LOCKWOOD, ISAAC	to Co. G.
PFEIFER, MAX W.	" G.

Co. "I."

This Company was organized at Bath, Steuben Co., N. Y., on the 26th day of June, 1846, and took its departure from that place on the 1st of August *en route* for Governor's Island, N. Y. Harbor. The "*Farmer's Advocate*" of Bath, under date of August 5th, 1846, says—"The Steuben Volunteers, under Captain Shannon, left Bath for New York on Saturday morning. We cannot refrain the repetition that we never saw a finer Company, all intelligent and vigorous young men, of many different trades, excellent habits, urbane manners and enterprising spirits. The mutual farewell echoed the best wishes and hopes, and a large number of our citizens volunteered carriages and escort to cheer them on board the Steuben steamer, which took its departure amid the acclamations of the mass of people assembled at the wharf." On the 26th day of September they left New York for California in the transport "Susan Drew" and arrived at San Francisco, on the 19th of March, 1847; from thence embarked on the "Lexington," in company with Companies "D," "E" and "I," and reached Monterey on the 4th of April, where the four companies went into camp on the green in front of the Catholic Church, which in honor of General Stephen W. Kearney (commanding the Military forces in California), was called "Camp Kearney." Upon the departure of Companies "E" and "G," for Los Angeles in the "Lexington" on the 5th of May—(Company "D" having been mounted were sent out to hunt for Indian horse thieves on the Tulare Plains), Company "I" took post at the barracks in the town. On the 28th of December the Company embarked on board the ———————and sailed for San Deigo, which place they continued to garrison until their discharge from the service on the 25th of September, 1848.

Co. "J."

Survivors, April 15th, 1882.

Lieut. PALMER B. HEWLETT .. .. Sonoma Co.
    Ex-Brig -Genl., National Guard State of California.
*EVANS, JOSEPH (Sergt.) .. .. Newark, N. J.
*EVANS, PLUMMER B. (Corpl.) .. .. Hampton, Va.
    Lieut. of Vols. late War.
*EMERSON, JOHN CALVIN, ... Bath, Steuben Co., N.Y.
*GUIBAL, EUGENE .. .. Gilroy.
HITT, CALVIN .. .. Winona, Minn.
*OSGOOD, HENRY M. .. San Luis Obispo.
SMITH, ELIJAH M. .. .. Aurora, Mono Co.
SULLIVAN, CORNELIUS .. Lompoc, Santa Barbara Co.
VINCENT, JOSHUA S. (Sergt.) .. Linn Creek, Camden Co., Mo.
*WARD, ANDREW J. .. Madison, Wis.
WOOD, JOHN .. .. .. Hanford, Tulare Co.
*SHARKEY, FRANK L. .. .. Norwich, Conn.

Supposed to be Living.

Lieut. HENRY MAGEE .. .. .. was at San Diego in 1874.
Lieut. WILLIAM H. SMITH was at Algerine Camp, Tuolumne Co., in 1874.
BUND, JOHN .. .. was on Calaveras River in 1874.
HARMON, DE WITT J. .. was at Murphy's, Calaveras Co., in 1874.
WYBOURN, ROBERT (Corpl.) .. .. was in Calaveras Co. in 1874.

Whereabouts Unknown.

BLACK, JAMES
BROOKS, EDWARD J.
CASEY, MICHAEL (Corpl.)
DOODY, PATRICK
GILLINGHAM, HENRY (Mus.)
HAUGHTY, MICHAEL
JOHNSON, IRA
KEMPST, GEORGE W.
KELLY, JAMES (Mus.)
KELLY, PHILIP

LUKER, WILLIAM
MAPES, WALTER B.
MORACE, ERASTUS
NICKERSON, THOMAS
PERRIN, JAMES
SMITH, CHARLES
SEXTON, LORIN
WIDGER, BENJAMIN
WITTAM, ISAAC
ZITTLE, MICHAEL

Deceased.

Capt. WILLIAM E. SHANNON .. .. Sacramento, Nov., 1850.
    Alcalde of Coloma District in 1849; Member of the Constitutional Convention at Monterey, 1849.
ALDRICH, JAMES .. .. City Point, Va., March 2, 1864.
BARNUM, EDGAR M. .. .. Monterey, Sept. 9, 1847.
BALDWIN, JOSIAH L. .. .. .. San Jose, Oct., 1850.
CLARK, JOHN N. .. Burrell Spring, Fresno Co., May 12, 1879.
CHASE, HIRAM .. .. Date and place unknown.

CONNELL, JOHN   at Sea, between California and Oregon.
DOMER, PETER ..   .. .. San Diego, June 24, 1848.
HARDMOUNT, WILLIAM ..   .. Date and place unknown.
KANE, PETER ..   .. Date and place unknown.
LOGAN, JOSEPH B. (Sergt.)   . Springfield, Tuolumne Co., Oct., 1857.
LOUNT, SETH H.   ..   Killed by Rogue River Indians in 1855.
MILLER, AUGUSTUS   .. Date and place unknown.
MURCH, WILLIAM B. (Corpl.)   .. Monterey, Oct. 27, 1847.
SHARP, MATTHEW W   .. .. near Coloma, in 1850.
SMITH, CHARLES F.   ..   ..   .. Date and place unknown.
STALL, ALFRED B...   ..   ..   .. Date and place unknown.
VAIL, JAMES M. Killed by Indians in Weaver Creek, El Dorado Co., in 1848.
VANKEUSEN, JEREMIAH   ..   ..   Aroca, N. Y., Sept., 1855.
WARBECK, HENRY R.   .. San Francisco, ——, 185—.
UNDERWOOD, G. L.   ..   .. Portland, Oregon, Nov. 15, 1881.
MAPES, GEORGE W.   .. .. Date and place unknown.

Transferred from Co. J.

Lieut. J. McH. HOLLINGSWORTH   . to Co. G.
ERATH, JOHN ..   ..   " G.
GRAFF, GEORGE J.   ..   ..   " E.
JACKSON, JAMES M.   ..   " G.
MOUSER, JOHN ..   " D.
SEARLES, GEORGE   " D.
SHIRLAND, E. D.   ..   " G.
STALL, ALFRED B.   :: G.

Co. "K."

This Company was recruited in Chenango County, N. Y., by Kimball H. Dimmick, a lawyer of Norwich, N. Y., who was subsequently elected captain. On the 3d of August, 1846, the Company left Chenango Co. for the rendezvous of the regiment on Governor's Island, at which place they arrived on the following morning. When the regiment embarked for California this Company was assigned to the transport "Loo Choo," arriving at San Francisco March 26th, 1847. Upon its arrival in California the Company was stationed at the Presidio, near San Francisco, at which post the Company remained on duty until its discharge from the service on the 15th of August, 1848.

Co. "K."

Survivors, April 15th, 1882.

*ABBOTT, AUSTIN R. (Corpl.)	Sacramento.
*CHRISTIAN, WILLIAM H.	.. Utica, N. Y.
Brig.-Genl. of Vols. late War.	
KNIGHT, JOHN	.. Ukiah.
MERRILL, JOHN H.	.. Washington, D. C.
MERRITT, ROBERT G.	Hopville, Mendocino Co.
O'NEIL, THOMAS	.. ———, Nevada.
RUGGLES, JOHN	Sacramento.
STOW, AARON	Davenport, Iowa.

Supposed to be Living.

REMINGTON, DARIUS C.	.. was at Washington Territory in 1874.
RODRIAN, CHARLES ..	.. .. was at San Francisco in 1874.
WALTHER, GEORGE	was at Los Angeles in 1874.

Whereabouts Unknown.

BROOKS, CHARLES W.	KELLY, JOHN
BANNARD, GEORGE	KOB, GEORGE
BRADY, JAMES	LEACH, FREDERICK N. (Mus.)
BROWNING, JOHN W.	LOUGHRAY, ANDREW
CROWLEY, MICHAEL	LOVELAND, CYRUS C.
CARTER, JOHN	McKAY, JOHN H.
DYE, HAZZARD	MAXWELL, JAMES W.
DURKUE, ANTHONY	MURRAY, EDWARD
FRINK, DANIEL	RAUSCH, NICHOLAS J.
FORRESTER, GEORGE H. H.	SELLERS, JACKSON (Sergt.)
FREEBORN, JOHN	SMITH, JAMES M.
GUILE, WILLIAM (Mus.)	STOPPARD, MOSES
GRAY, WILLIAM D.	SLEIGHT, PETER
HUDSON, BENJAMIN	WHITE, PHILANDER (Corpl.)
HOYT, DANIEL C.	WILKES, JOHN
HUNTLEY, EZRA	WOOLARD, HENRY
JOHNSON, CHARLES F.	WHEELOCK, LYMAN
KENDALL, ALVA	WEIDNEY, ANTHONY
KLOPPER, MICHAEL	WHEELER, JOHN

Deceased.

Capt. KIMBALL H. DIMMICK	Date and place unknown.

Member of the State Constitutional Convention at Monterey, 1849. Appointed by Gov. B. Riley, Judge First Superior Tribunal of Cal., Nov. 1, 1849.

Lieut. JOHN S. NORRIS	in Central America in 1856.
Lieut. GEORGE C. HUBBARD	.. ———Illinois,——— 185—
Lieut. RODERICK M. MORRISON	at Carson Creek, April 18, 1849.

CAMPBELL, WILLIAM .. .. .. San Jose, Dec. 18, 1848.
CALLENDER, MILLS L. .. Brooklyn, N. Y., Feb. 21, 1871.
HOMMITCH, JOHN .. San Francisco, Dec. 26, 1876.
LIVINGSTON, PETER F. Sonora, Tuolumne Co., Sept. 30, 1873.
MARCH, EDWIN .. Pleasant Springs, Nov. 2d. 1860.
NEEB, JOHN Sonoma, Feb. 20, 1874.
SISSON, RUEBEN (Corp'l) .. Mission, San Rafael, Nov. 30, 1849.
WILLIAMSON, THOMAS DENT * **Santa Rosa, Sonoma Co., —— 187—**

Transferred from Co. R.

Lieut. THERON R. PER LEE .. .. to Co. C.
†Lieut. GEORGE, D. BREWERTON .. to 1st U. S. Dragoons.
AMES, THADDEUS M. .. .. to Co. C.
FORBES, ELI B. .. .. " F.
MILLER, VALENTINE to Regimental Band.
PFIESTER, ADOLPH .. .. " "

* Now a resident of Brooklyn, N. Y.

Chaplain.

Rev. T. M. LEAVENWORTH .. .. now residing in Sonoma Co.

RECAPITULATION.

	Survivors	Supposed to be Living	Whereabouts Unknown	Deceased	TOTAL
Field Officers............	1	—	—	2	3
Staff Officers...........	6	—	—	1	7
Captains...............	5	—	—	4	9
Lieutenants............	7	3	4	16	30
Non-Commissioned Staff.	—	—	—	4	4
Regimental Band.......	—	—	16	5	21
Non-Com. Officers and Privates............	136	30	423	181	770
	155	33	443	213	844

The ten companies comprising the Regiment were mustered out of the service of the United States, as follows:

BY LIEUT. JAS. A. HARDIE (Late Major of the Regiment),
3d U. S. Artillery.

Company "C," Capt. J. E. Brackett,
at San Francisco, August 15th, 1848.
Company "K," Capt. K. H. Dimmick,
at San Francisco, August 15th, 1848.
Company "H," Capt. J. B. Frisbie,
at San Francisco, August 25th, 1848.

BY CAPT. A. J. SMITH,
1st U. S. Dragoons.

Company "F," Capt. F. J. Lippitt,
at Santa Barbara, September 8th, 1848.
Company "E," Capt. Nelson Taylor,
at Los Angeles, September 18th, 1848.
Company "G," Capt. M. R. Stevenson,
at Los Angeles, September 18th, 1848.
Company "I," Capt. W. E. Shannon,
at San Diego, September 25th, 1848.

BY CAPT. HENRY S. BURTON (late Lieut. Col. of the Regiment),
3d U. S. Artillery.

Company "A," Capt. S. G. Steele,
at Monterey, October 23d, 1848.
Company "B," Lieut. H. C. Mattsell,
at Monterey, October 23d, 1848.
Company "D," Capt. H. M. Naglee,
at Monterey, October 24th, 1848.

The Field Officers of the Regiment were mustered out of service by Capt. H. S. Burton, at Monterey, Cal., October 26th, 1848.

THE TRANSPORT FLEET

The following named vessels conveyed the Regiment to California, and the information relative to their subsequent career has been kindly furnished by the "*Sun Mutual Insurance Company of New York*," as also the "*Atlantic Mutual Insurance Company of New York.*"

Ship "THOMAS H. PERKINS," 697 tons burden, Arthur, Master, with Companies B, F, G, and a portion of Co. E, Col. J. D. Stevenson commanding troops.

This ship was sold during the late civil war to a merchant of London, England; name changed to the "Anstruther" of London. On the 5th day of December, 1872, this vessel was at Pensacola, Florida.

Ship "LOO CHOO," 639 tons burden, Jas. B. Hatch, Master, with Companies A, C, K, and a portion of Co. E, Major Jas. A. Hardie, commanding troops.

This ship was at New York in 1865, no trace of vessel since that date.

Ship "SUSAN DREW," 701 tons burden, Putnam, Master, with Companies D, I, H, and a portion of Co. E, Lieut. Col. Henry S. Burton commanding troops.

This ship was sold to British owners, name changed to "Magdalena," and sailed from San Francisco, February 4th, 1852, for Panama; in April, 1852, she was reported at Panama.

Ship "BRUTUS," 463 tons burden, Adams, Master, sailed from New York November 13th, 1846, with the officers and men who were left at New York at the date of the sailing of the Regiment; Capt. Nelson Taylor, of Co. E, commanding detachment.

This vessel was last recorded as lying in the port of New York in the month of July, 1860; for the three years previous she had been on a whaling voyage. No record of the vessel can be traced since that date.

Ship "ISABELLA," 649 tons burden, Geo. Briggs, Master, sailed from Philadelphia on the 19th day of August, 1847, with 100 recruits for the Regiment, in charge of Lieut. Thomas J Roach.

The "Isabella" was sold in 1863 to parties of Liverpool, England, name changed to "Lilla Mansfield;" the year following her sale and change of flag she was wrecked on the coast of Ireland.

Ship "SWEDEN," 616 tons burden, Knott, Master, sailed from New York in the month of September, 1847, with 100 recruits for the Regiment, in charge of Lieut. Thomas E. Ketchum.

This vessel put into Gibraltar while on a voyage from Leghorn to Philadelphia in the month of January, 1860 (another report says April, 1860), was there condemned as unseaworthy.

The following interesting article is from the pen of Col. Thos. Crosby Lancey, of San Francisco:—

THE history of the causes which led to and the manner in which the acquisition of California was made by the United States are at this date almost unknown to perhaps the majority of the people who now dwell in this State. To many the events of the years before the great influx of the gold seeking population who came here in 1849-50 have been unrevealed, and even to those who have been cognizant of the thrilling drama enacted here, the remembrance has all but faded out. The story of those brave and adventurous spirits who—long before the cry of gold reached the East, borne upon the winds that blew over the Sierras from ocean to ocean—conceived and carried out the idea of adding California, then a province of Mexico, as another jewel to the star en-crowned United States, has never yet been given to the world in its completeness, and so to-day, grateful Californians know not to whom they are indebted for their fair heritage. Without seeking to wrest a single laurel from the many gallant men who were here before the war with Mexico (in 1846) broke out, the "Post" must concede to the famous Stevenson's Regiment, which arrived in this State from New York during that period, a generous share of the honors of the conquest. The causes which led to the formation of that command; the trials of its commander in selecting suitable men; the purposes for which it was organized; its sailing; the voyage, and landing here—all of these are interesting facts. When the war with Mexico broke out Colonel Stevenson was a member of the New York Legislature, on the closing session of which he made a speech warmly supporting the Government in its action. Soon after Colonel Stevenson had business in Washington City, where he called upon his old friend, Amos Kendall, then Post Master-General. At the house of the latter he was introduced to a prominent Mormon, who had just secured permission from President Polk to organize a regiment at Council Bluffs to march to California under the command of a United States officer. During the conversation Colonel Stevenson remarked that he had heard much of California, and would like very much to go there. Mr. Kendall in reporting the matter of the organizing of the Mormon regiment, incidentally mentioned that Colonel Stevenson was in the city, and also mentioned what he said relative to California. The

President immediately said to Mr. Kendall: "See Colonel Stevenson, and tell him that if he is disposed to go to California I will give him authority to raise a regiment of New York volunteers." Colonel Stevenson was informed of this offer by Mr. Kendall, and soon after Gen. J. A. Dix, then Senator from New York, also came to his hotel, and told him the President had asked his opinion regarding the idea of sending a detachment by way of Cape Horn. He approved of the measure and of the commander chosen, as, had he the nomination, he would name Col. Stevenson before any other citizen soldier that he knew. Hon. Daniel S. Dickinson, also a Senator from New York, likewise tendered his congratulations to Colonel Stevenson, and wished him success. Colonel Stevenson felt much delicacy in calling upon the President, and therefore delayed doing so until he should receive an invitation from him. The next day, after Secretary Marcy had told him of what President Polk had said, Colonel Stevenson visited the mansion grounds, where on one day in each week, a grand out of door musical soiree was given by the band, which generally attracted some 5,000 people, and while there a servant approached with a request from President Polk who was on the rear portico, that the Colonel should step around and see him. The Colonel did so, and the President in person requested him to call upon him the next day. In the interview on the following day the President questioned Colonel Stevenson closely as to his previous pursuits and his experience in business. These the Colonel answered satisfactorily, and then the President added that he had heard him spoken very highly of as a commander and a man of ability by Secretary of War Marcy and others, said that he was satisfied he would do honor to himself in the matter, and thereupon gave him authority to raise the regiment. Colonel Stevenson then left the executive chamber with orders to the Secretary of the Navy, Quartermaster and Commissary General for the necessary arms, supplies and transportation of the regiment. The Cabinet approved of the appointment of Colonel Stevenson, and heartily entertained the idea of the conquest of California. Gen. Winfield Scott, who was also present, thought the appointment a good one, and assented to it. Col. Stevenson then left for New York, and in the morning the mail brought him the official permission to raise the regiment, signed by W. L. Marcy, and dated June 26, 1846. The instructions from the Secretary were that the regiment should be composed of unmarried men, of good habits and varied pursuits, and such as would be likely to remain in California or adjoining territory at the close of the war. It was understood that the recruits must be informed that they were to go a long distance, and that they were to enlist for the war and no shorter length of time, and that they also might be mustered out of service at any point within the United States that the commandant named at the conclusion of the war. The notification also read that the command would be expected to start early in August, 1846. Upon receipt of this Colonel Stevenson, in a communication dated June 30th, wrote to Silas Wright, the Governor of New York, for the necessary permission to raise a regiment in the State. To this the Governor graciously consented. Up to this time nothing was known of the intended movement, and Colonel Stevenson himself had the pleasure of announcing it at the usual gathering of all the officers of the citizen soldiery of the city of New York, at the Governor's room, upon the 4th of July, 1846. The following day the newspapers contained full accounts of the new movement, and on the 7th of July Colonel Stevenson took up his head-quarters at the old State Arsenal in White street, and began receiving recruits for the seven companies to be raised in New York City, which, with three companies to be recruited in the interior of the State, would make ten companies of a regiment of 1,000 men. Colonel Stevenson had arranged that his own commission, as well as those of his staff, should be issued by the State of New York, and he also had determined that his field and staff should, if possible, be composed of officers of the regular army or graduates of West Point. His reason for desiring that his principal officers should be graduates of West Point was that he intended to bring the regiment out in three detachments, and he wanted able men to command and drill them. Colonel Stevenson had especially requested the Secretary of War not to appoint any one to accompany him, except in a military capacity, and then not unless he was under his control. As soon as it became generally known that a regiment was to be raised for service in California numerous applications for positions were made to the President and Secretary of War, all of which were referred to Colonel Stevenson. Many applications were made for the positions of Surgeon and Assistant-Surgeon to the regiment. The applications were referred to the United States Board of Medical Examiners, who recommended Alexander Perry for Surgeon and William C

Parker for Assistant-Surgeon. Colonel Stevenson, having succeeded in getting the officers of his choice for the field and staff, felt assured of the success of the expedition, and at once turned his attention to the organization of the several companies. The various officers recruiting these companies had been given full and special instructions, and in a very short time ten full companies of splendid men had been recruited, seven of which were from New York, one from Albany and the other two from the interior counties of the State. These companies were on the 1st of August gathered together in general encampment on Governor's Island, N. Y. Harbor, the tents being pitched on a lawn between Fort Columbus and Castle Williams. Here, on the first day of August, 1846, the regiment was mustered into service by Colonel Bankhead, commanding the Second Regiment of Artillery, as the *Seventh* New York Volunteers.

There were 38 commissioned officers and 729 non-commissioned officers and privates, making a total of 767, rank and file.

The regulations of the service provided that all recruits should be surgically examined within four days of their application, but at that time the examining physicians were so busy elsewhere that it was not until the 20th of August that the Regiment was examined. So strict were the examining surgeons that out of the 800 men there, 150 were rejected. When it became known that so many had been rejected, over 500 applications were made for the vacancies within two days. Very few members of the Regiment were over twenty-one years of age, and no married men, excepting those whose wives accompanied the regiment as laundresses, were taken. Some of these rejected men were very bitter against Colonel Stevenson, and talked of suing him for false imprisonment in keeping them on Governor's Island for twenty odd days without having them examined, but when the matter was fully explained to them a greater portion at once saw that he was not to blame, and relinquished the idea.

At about this time one Thomas Jefferson Sutherland, who had in earlier days organized a band of men to co-operate with some discontented spirits in Canada, who were trying to create a revolution there, appeared on the scene. This Sutherland, during the trouble mentioned, had gathered about 100 men, and had taken possession of Navy Island, in the Niagara river, above the Falls, and so alarmed the Canadians that they requested the

United States to remove them. This was accordingly done by a detachment of United States soldiery. From that time until the breaking out of the war with Mexico he led a wandering, vagabond life, and when he heard of Colonel Stevenson's intended departure he applied to the Secretary of War for a position in that Regiment. The Secretary directed him to Colonel Stevenson, without, however, recommending him, or even giving him a note to the Colonel on the subject. A few days after he appeared before Colonel Stevenson, at Governor's Island, and, although a perfect stranger to him asked for a position on his staff. When told there was no vacancy, he, with a sublimity of cheek truly refreshing, said that while he would prefer going as a military man, still he would accept the position of "adviser" to Colonel Stevenson, which position he could fill with ability, owing to his great military experience. Upon the Colonel's refusing the proffered counsel, Sutherland waxed indignant, and saucily told that gentleman that he had much powerful influence, and that he (the Colonel) would be made to feel the weight of his displeasure, before the command left, if, indeed, he did not entirely prevent its departure. At this the patience of Colonel Stevenson, became exhausted, and he ordered him from the tent and off the camp ground. Nothing more was heard of the would-be "adviser" until, some fifteen days before the time appointed for the command to sail, the Colonel received a communication from the Secretary of War, inclosing a communication from some prominent politicians of Philadelphia to President Polk, advising him that matters were so shaping at New York that Colonel Stevenson might be prevented from going to California in command of the expedition, and that in case he did not go all of his field officers would resign on account of their attachment to him. The communication also went on to say that they would recommend for the Colonel's position a certain captain in the New York volunteers, and graduate of West Point. This communication, although coming without a word of comment, created quite a disturbance in Col. Stevenson's mind, and he set himself to work carefully reviewing his whole life, to see if he could find aught objectionable that his bitterest enemy could point to with scorn or contempt. Although in his forty-sixth year, he could find nothing in his whole life, nearly all of which had been passed in New York, which he could not justify before the whole community. Feeling assured also of the respect and friendship of both the

President and Secretary of War, he immediately telegraphed the latter that the command would sail on the 25th or 26th of September. Preparations for departure were hurried to completion.

The ships Thomas H. Perkins, Loo Choo, and Susan Drew, having been chartered by the Secretary of War and their lower holds filled with naval stores, munitions of war, grist and saw mills, and everything that was considered necessary for the conquest and retention of California, were only awaiting the embarkation of the troops to sail.

A meeting of the junior commanders with their superiors was held the day after the dispatch had been sent, which was on the 23d of September, and then Colonel Stevenson informed them of his determination to sail on the 25th. To this the officers demurred, they arguing that both the soldiers and sailors, being superstitious, would be greatly dissatisfied sailing on a Friday. Finally, these unexpected objections having due weight, the Colonel made the day of sailing one day later. This arrangement was to be kept an entire secret from both the line officers, soldiers, and the sailors. The conference then adjourned. At its close a young friend of the Colonel's, for whom he had secured a position in the Sheriff's office, New York, came into the tent laboring under much suppressed excitement, and began revealing a most dastardly and cunningly-contrived plot designed to prevent Colonel Stevenson from accompanying his Regiment. This young man, whom the Colonel had benefitted so much, had not forgotten his benefactor, and now, when he found opportunity to do him a service, it was eagerly embraced. The startling intelligence that he brought was that some seventy or eighty of the discontented rejected applicants previously mentioned had been induced by some influence to bring suits for false imprisonment against Colonel Stevenson, the damages claimed aggregating $80,000. The young man begged Colonel Stevenson not to reveal his informant's name, for if he did it would result in his losing his place. The whole matter was held as a secret in the Sheriff's office. In this the Colonel thought he discerned the work of the artful Sutherland and his Pennsylvania friends, and at once asked his informant if he had ever seen Sutherland in the Sheriff's office. He answered that he had, and that an officer of Colonel Stevenson's regiment had also been seen there. The writs of attachments in these suits were all ready to be served, and the Sheriff's officers were only waiting for the actual day of sailing to serve them upon the defendant. Having placed his friend upon the look-out the young man bade him adieu, after promising that if anything new transpired he would inform him of it. Immediately after the departure of his young friend orders were issued to break camp and to embark, and by nine o'clock on Thursday morning, the 24th, the entire command was aboard the transports, and the commander of the squadron's flag floated at the masthead of the Colonel's ship, where he had his head-quarters. The first order issued on shipboard was that no one should be permitted to board or leave the ship, except by the written permission of the commanding officer. On Wednesday, after making all the arrangements for embarking, the Colonel sent word to his motherless daughters, residing at home, in Rutger's place, to meet him at twelve o'clock that night at the house of Frank Geroe, a friend in Brooklyn, to bid him good-by, as he would be unable to visit his home before sailing. Shortly before that hour the Colonel stepped into his boat, manned by six trusty men and a coxswain, all armed, including the Colonel, with pistols and cutlasses, and gave orders to pull for Brooklyn. The night being dark and the oars having been muffled the boat reached Brooklyn unobserved, and Colonel Stevenson had the pleasure of being with his three daughters for an hour, when he bade them a fond and an affectionate farewell. The parting was most painful, but the young ladies, being cast in a heroic mold, strove to hide their feelings of sorrow from their sire and not add to his keen grief. Fondly and lovingly he kissed them good-by, then hastened to leave the soil of New York, which he has never since then set foot upon, and board his vessel. After the command had been gotten aboard the greatest precautions were at once taken to prevent any of the Sheriff's employes from serving any writs upon Colonel Stevenson. The Colonel's boat, with four well-armed men in it, was stationed at the foot of the rope ladder, and orders were given that any person wanting to come on board should send up his card and business from this boat, and if any one attempted to force his way on board he should be seized and ironed.

Men were also stationed at four different parts of the vessel with a 32 pound shot within reach, with orders to sink any boat that persisted in making fast to the vessel after being ordered off. Several attempts were made by the Sheriff's officers to get on board to serve their writs, by means of sending up false messages, giving other than their own names, and other devices, not one of which deceived the grim Colonel, who was not to be caught with chaff. One party made a forcible attempt to get aboard, but a **shot** dropped between their boat and the ship by a guard, who immediately seized another shot, as if to be more accurate, caused the adventurous craft to hastily pull away. All day Thursday and Friday this strict guard was **kept up. On Thursday afternoon** Colonel Stevenson called an old man-of-war's-man into **his cabin,** and, knowing that he **could rely upon him,** explained the situation to him, and placed him in charge of **the ship's cannon, with instruction** to select a corps to **man each gun and to see that the** cannons were **carefully loaded** with **grape and** cannister and kept **ready for instant service. Through** the Quartermaster at New **York, Colonel Stevenson had** ordered four steamers (tug-boats **were** then unknown) to be in readiness to tow the flotilla out at **a** given signal, which was to **be** two cannon shots in quick succession. These orders were given the captains of the steamers under the promise of secrecy, and no other soul on them knew of the duty they were to perform. Friday was, perhaps, the most **anxious day** of Colonel Stevenson's life. Still it is doubtful if living man could have learned it from his immobile features, calm **voice or** undisturbed **manner.** He gave audience to many of his friends, transacted **business with others, and at half-past two** closed his audience for **the day and went on deck to make** arrangements for doubling guards. Gathering a few of his trusty friends about him he explained the situation to them also, and told them that he **intended to resist arrest at all** hazards, even if the Sheriff's boat had to be blown out **of the water. At about three o'clock** a small steamer was sighted coming down East river, and apparently heading for the vessel. As she approached **nearer and nearer** the Colonel called **Captain** Turner's attention to it, and instructed him, in case she attempted to come alongside, to hail her and notify the man at the wheel that if he did **not keep off** he would be **shot** dead where he stood.

A young German, formerly a soldier in the Prussian army, prompt and faithful, was placed in an advantageous position, and these orders given: At the word "Ready!" he was to raise his **piece—which,** with but a cap on it, combined with the snap of **the lock,** made a report loud as a derringer—and cock it. At the **word "**Aim!" he was to bring down his piece and to draw a bead upon the man in the pilot-house of the approaching steamer. All these directions were given the man in a loud tone, and could be distinctly heard on board the steamer. A tinkle of the bell, and she slowed down to come alongside, driven by her acquired force. Just then the officer of the day gave the sentinel the command of "Ready!" and up went the gun, the cocking of which sounded clear and determined. The order to aim immediately followed, when Captain Turner sung out to the steamer's pilot: "I will give you five seconds to back your steamer; if she does not move you are a dead man!" The pilot looked but one second at the captain, another second was taken in glancing down that threatening gun barrel, and then clang went the bell, and the wheels of the steamer began rapidly to back water, and she moved off as quickly and as silently as she came, the man at the wheel not taking his eyes off that terrible gun until he was well out of range. That was the last attempt made to arrest Colonel Stevenson on that day. That evening he notified Captain Shields of the United States sloop of war "Preble," which vessel was to accompany his command, that he should sail early the following morning, the 26th, and also gave him a dispatch to be sent the President and Secretary of War containing the same notification. That same evening Colonel Stevenson sent a messenger to notify the steamers he had engaged to be alongside at daylight to tow him out, and also to tell Deputy Sheriff A. M. C. Smith, who was on the steamer which attempted to come alongside of the "Perkins" that afternoon, that he (Colonel Stevenson) would never be arrested in that harbor, and that he intended to leave at the head of his command, peaceably if he could, forcibly if he must. The deputy then said to the messenger that the Sheriff was out of town. He had been telegraphed the failure to arrest Colonel Stevenson, and had replied that he would return to the city by eight o'clock the next morning. The return of the messenger with this report quieted Colonel Stevenson's apprehensions, and he turned in, hoping that he could leave New York without bloodshed. At dawn on the 26th he was up and on deck awaiting the coming steamers. While thus waiting, an answer to the telegram sent to the President and Secretary of War was received. It read as follows: "Your telegram received. Our answer is, God bless and speed you safely to your new home;" signed by President Polk and Secretary Marcy.

While this was being read, Robert Martin, news collector for the *New York Herald*, and personal friend of Colonel Stevenson, came on board, bringing with him the State flag and two guide colors, parts of a stand of colors that the officers of Colonel Stevenson's old militia regiment that he had commanded for twenty years, learning that the fleet was about to sail, had sent on board. Colonel Stevenson received the colors with thanks, and taking leave of Martin, gave orders to weigh anchor, and in a few moments, the steamers having come along side, the little flotilla began moving out down the Narrows. Just at this moment, as Colonel Stevenson was looking through his glass, at the immense concourse of people gathered on the Battery, he saw a large column of men moving along pier No. 1 to the steamer lying at the end of the pier. This he correctly surmised to be a Sheriff's posse to arrest him. Towing the "Perkins," which had all sails set, were two powerful steamers, and with the advantage of an ebb tide it was hoped that she could not be overtaken. As the fleet passed out the Narrows, Fort Lafayette saluted and the ships responded. As the smoke of the canonading cleared away, the little steamer with the Sheriff's posse on board was seen rounding Governor's Island. She did not continue the chase long, for when the fleet rounded Sandy Hook naught could be seen of her, even through a glass. At about five miles out Colonel Stevenson signalled the vessels to heave to, and taking one of the steamers, visited in succession each one of them, bidding good-by to his captains, and leaving orders with them to rendezvous at Rio de Janeiro. When the steamer ranged alongside the "Susan Drew," he noticed that the officer intended as his successor by the Philadelphia politicians, and the same who had been seen at the Sheriff's office was in the mizzen chains, to be the first to have a parting clasp of the hands with Colonel Stevenson, who, however, in boarding, did not choose to notice his extended hand. When, however, this gentleman placed his hand in his, Colonel Stevenson looked him steadily in the eye. The officer at that glance flushed guiltily, and knew then that the Colonel was aware of his perfidy towards him. Slowly the checkmated villain withdrew his hand and slunk away.

As a final salute, each of the ships manned the yards and their crews gave three vigorous cheers; then all sail was spread, and thus the Regiment left New York for the far western shore. When it is remembered that this was the first army ever sent by the United States to subjugate and occupy a foreign territory, and that never before in the history of the world did a detachment of soldiers go so far to reach the enemy's country, the event becomes one of great historical interest. As the returning steamers faded from view, the brave and undaunted commander sought the solitude of his cabin, where, kneeling, he devoutly thanked his Creator for aiding him safely through the troubles of the few days past.

Always a sufferer from sea-sickness when at sea, Colonel Stevenson, admonished by premonitory symptoms of that unwelcome visitor, as the "Perkins" lost sight of land, hastened to make all preparation to resign himself, with as good grace as possible, to its consequences. Every part of the vessel was visited and orders given the officers for a week ahead. None too soon were these precautions taken, for Colonel Stevenson had the inevitable attack which confined him to his state-room for three days, and when he reappeared on deck he was but the ghost of his former self, and was so weak that for many days he had to be supported by two sturdy soldiers. Others of the command also suffered from the same infliction. Another of the evils of a long voyage is scurvy. This was well guarded against, however, great care being taken that plenty of wholesome food, and in variety, should be served out. The result of this was that nothing of the kind appeared. All the officers messed together, with the exception of the master of the ship, Captain Arthur. This officer, an eccentric personage, was a German by birth, but he had mingled so freely with the people of all nations, that his nationality was a matter of speculation. He was also most penurious and ill tempered, and when out of humor, which happened often, he was perfectly unbearable.

Previous to sailing, he asked permission to join the officers' mess, adding that he could purchase a supply of pigs, chickens and ducks, cheaper than its members could. The proposition was acceded to, and the captain proceeded to lay in much live stock and poultry. He, however, delayed joining the mess until well out to sea, and when, about a week after sailing, it was proposed that he should unite with the mess, and that the event should be celebrated by a chicken dinner, he cooly informed the astonished officers that he had changed his mind, and had concluded not to join the mess. If they wanted any chickens, however, he would sell the mess any number at fair prices. The officers, disgusted at his conduct, did not press him to join the mess, but they bartered for his chickens. Here again they were astonished, for the price asked for the chickens was fully three times that which he had paid for them, so they concluded not to purchase, consigning both the captain and his fowls to hades. This unexpected determination on the part of his intended victims proved unfortunate for the petty speculator; for, the soldiers and crew, learning the trick he had served the officers, also declined to buy a single fowl from him. This was not the extent of his loss, either; for, although he did not sell a chicken, he soon witnessed them rapidly disappear, owing to numerous midnight raids, until at last not a feather of them was left. The young and succulent pigs, too, grew so large and fat, that they had to be killed and salted down. No other instance of pilfering on the part of the command was recorded on the voyage. During the passage the best of discipline was maintained, and there were few violations of the rules. The command, with one exception, paid strict attention to them. This exception was a sergeant of one of the companies. An order had been issued that each soldier should be in his bunk by nine o'clock, ready to turn in at the tap of the drum. This sergeant, in giving the order to his detachment, supplemented it with the remark, "I have given you the order and I don't care a —— whether you obey it or not." This remark was repeated to Colonel Stevenson, who at once reduced the man to the ranks and detailed him for police duty, which was to clean up the ship. This duty he refused to perform, and so he was ordered triced up by the thumbs and wrists; and the order was also given to keep him in that position until he was ready to make a proper apology for his conduct. This he refused to do, and when his captain tried to reason with him he cursed and swore like a pirate. He was then left alone to come to his senses, but was visited hourly by the ship's surgeon, who, from time to time, reported on his physical condition.

As might have been expected, the punishment of the fractious sergeant caused a murmur of discontent forward, until at length, seeking to frighten Colonel Stevenson into relaxing his severity, Captain Folsom, who had before presumed on his superior's friendship, entered his cabin and in rather an insolent manner said to him: "Colonel Stevenson, do you know that there will be a mutiny on this vessel this afternoon?"

"No, sir," replied Colonel Stevenson, "but I do know that there will not be a mutiny on board this ship this afternoon; and further, Captain Folsom, you know that I sleep over nine hundred tons of gunpowder, but you do not know, sir, that I have a train laid from that powder to my berth?"

"What?" stammered the captain. "Colonel Stevenson, you surely do not mean to say——"

"Yes, sir, I do, and you can rest assured that before I will suffer the command of this vessel to pass from me there will not be a plank left for a soul on board to cling to; and now, sir, let the mutiny proceed!"

Pale as a spectre, and with his eyes fairly emerging from their sockets, the thoroughly alarmed officer hastily excused himself and hurried forward, where he, no doubt, imparted the fearful threat he had just heard to the malcontents waiting there, who, if they had ever entertained mutinous ideas, quickly discarded them. The feeling of discontent, however, was not crushed. At roll call that evening, and while the men, mustered on deck, were being inspected, the soldier undergoing punishment moaned as if in pain. At this his bunk-mate, who was standing in line close by, brought his piece to the deck in a forcible manner and exclaimed, "By G—, I would like to see the man that would serve me—" whack came a blow, given quick as lightning by Colonel Stevenson, who, in passing, had caught the sentence ere it was finished, and, with a thud, the mutinous soldier fell doubled up in a heap upon the deck. Then calmly ordering a sergeant to incarcerate the fallen man in the ship's prison and keep him on bread and water for ten days, Colonel Stevenson quietly proceeded with the inspection. This display of courage and firmness had a wholesome effect on the discontented men and on the triced-up sergeant, who soon after sent word to Colonel Stevenson that he was anxious to make the apology demanded, and, on that officer's appearing, did so most humbly. He was then released, and from that time on both he and the rest of the rebellious spirits behaved themselves as well as the most orderly of the command. Thus ended the mutiny predicted by Captain Folsom.

The next event of any importance was the birth of a female child. This was born to the wife of Quartermaster-Sergeant Stephen Harris. On the same day, also, the "Perkins" fell in with her convoy, the sloop "Preble," Captain Shields. The officers and crew of this vessel, on learning of the infantile arrival, requested permission to name the little stranger, which, being granted, the name of Alta California was chosen for her, and so three vigorous cheers were given for little Miss Alta California Harris by both ships' crews. A few days later, on the 20th of

November, the two vessels having in the meantime parted company, the " Perkins " entered the bay of Rio de Janeiro, where the "Susan Drew," the " Loo Choo " and the " Preble" were found to have arrived and were at anchor. Here was also the United States man-of-war, "Columbia," flagship of Commodore Rosseau, commanding the Brazilian Squadron. When the " Perkins' dropped anchor all the vessels manned yards and saluted in man-of-war style. Shortly after, an officer was sent from the " Perkins " to report to Commodore Rosseau, who soon afterwards visited Colonel Stevenson. The " Perkins " was also boarded by the Brazilian authorities, who requested that the commander of the " Perkins " would honor them by exchanging salutes with their forts. Their exchange of courtesies was agreed upon, to take place the following day. A communication received soon after from Commodore Rosseau, however, made it necessary to cancel the arrangement. This communication was to the effect that owing to a difficulty between the Brazilian Government and Hon. H. A. Wise, United States Minister at Rio de Janeiro, all diplomatic intercourse between the two nations had been suspended. The communication ended by saying that as Colonel Stevenson commanded an independent expedition, he could act as he pleased in the matter. That commander, without hesitation, resolved to support Minister Wise, and so sent a messenger ashore to the Brazilian officials to say that it would not be desirable to exchange salutes as agreed upon. The following day the United States officers in port in a body, upon invitation, visited tne various foreign Embassies in that city, but no notice was taken of the Brazilian officials.

This slight did not serve to mollify the people of Brazil in the least, and the breach was further widened in the christening of the protege of the expedition,which took place the next day. Extensive preparations were made for that event. The officers of the " Preble " selected an elegant silver cup, suitably engraved, and issued invitations to all of the United States officials to attend the christening of Miss Alta California Harris, to take place on board the " Columbia," the fleet chaplain officiating. The vessel selected was gaily decorated for the occasion, and, at the hour set, all invited were present to participate in the honor to be done the daughter of an humble soldier of a great republic. All were aware that the child was born famous, for was she not the first child ever born whose father formed part of the first expedition of armed

5

American emigrant soldiers ever sent by their Government to conquer and occupy a foreign province? Minister Wise was to stand god-father, and he and the child's parents, Commodore Rosseau, Colonel Stevenson and the chaplain, occupied a central position on the deck. The interesting ceremony was performed and Minister Wise followed in a speech. Unfortunately, in concluding, he drew a comparison between the christening of a daughter of an American soldier and a similar event which had taken place on shore a few days previous in which the "royal bantling of the Brazilian Nation," as he termed the child, had been the principal. The ceremony on the "Columbia" was concluded by hearty cheering and the firing of salutes from every vessel in the fleet. The insult—so regarded—offered by Minister Wise, coming to the knowledge of the Court of Brazil, a cabinet meeting was called and the question of ordering every American vessel out of the port was debated. Learning of this proposed action, Colonel Stevenson visited first the most distant vessel of his fleet, and in a speech to the officers and men, countermanded the order allowing a portion of the command liberty on shore each day, and explaining matters, said that he expected that Commodore Rosseau would refuse to obey the order. In that case it would be his duty to stand by him, and that a conflict between their vessels and the vessels and batteries of Brazil would be inevitable. That being the case, he said that the next time they went ashore it would be with fixed bayonets. This announcement had an electrical effect upon the men. They jumped into the rigging and uttered cheer after cheer. Those on the nearest vessel, while not understanding the cause of the outburst, became excited also, and they, too, joined in the enthusiastic hurrah. And thus, from vessel to vessel, cheer followed cheer, and when Colonel Stevenson was rowed to each ship in turn, and they also were told the news, the men, knowing the cause of the outburst, cheered louder than before. All this time the scene on shore was of the liveliest nature.

Upon the quay fully 20,000 people had gathered, curious to know what the Americans were growing so demonstrative about. Then, after waiting till the excitement had subsided on shipboard, the swarming piers gradually grew less crowded, until finally the docks resumed their wonted appearance. A few hours after Commodore Rosseau thanked Colonel Stevenson, in person, for his proffered aid, and told him that he (Colonel Stevenson) had interpreted correctly what his action would be in case the decree was made. No such summary step as contemplated by the Brazilian authorities was ever taken, for the Emperor of Brazil opposed the issuance of such an order, but insisted on demanding the recall of Minister Wise by the United States Government, which demand was subsequently acceded to. A careful and complete report of his own action in the affair was forwarded the Secretary of War by Colonel Stevenson, an acknowledgment, without comment, of the receipt of which was duly received by him when he arrived in California. A few days after this episode the sailing orders were given to the fleet, and the four vessels once again breasted the ocean with all sail set, bound round the Horn. Nothing further of importance transpired on board the "Perkins" during the remainder of the voyage. The health and discipline of the Command were perfect. Favored with fair weather and fresh breezes the good ship rapidly neared her destination, until in the latter part of February, 1847, the welcome shores of California appeared in the horizon. A few days sail along the coast brought the vessel off the heads, and on the 6th of March, 1847, the "Perkins" sailed proudly through the Golden Gate, and at three o'clock rounded to and came to an anchor opposite the little town of Yerba Buena. The United States sloop-of-war, "Cyane," Captain Dupont, was in the harbor, and from its officers Colonel Stevenson learned that the town was held by a detachment of the United States Marine Corps, under Lieutenant Tansell. General Stephen W. Kearney, commanding the Department of the Pacific was at Monterey, and to him Colonel Stevenson sent a courier announcing his arrival.

The "Perkins," "Loo Choo," and "Susan Drew" reached Rio de Janeiro the same day, Nov. 20, and sailed together on the 29th; at Rio de Janeiro, Captain James M. Turner resigned and returned home, and in the "Loo Choo," off Cape Horn, First Lieut. William R. Tremmels died. The "Perkins" reached San Francisco, March 6, 1847, 165 days from N. Y., having lost four by death and gained two by birth. The "Susan Drew" reached San Francisco March 19, 1847. The "Loo Choo" struck a calm near the tropics which lengthened her passage, and it was during this calm that the poet of the ship wrote these lines which were published in the early papers of San Francisco. I only remember the following line,

"The old Loo Choo seemed dreaming
So idly did she lay."

The following, which was written on board, Feb. 25, 1847, setting forth the objects of this visit to California, will be, I think, welcomed by all the survivors of that Regiment.

COLUMBIA'S GREETING TO CALIFORNIA.

BY W. M., FIRST REG'T N. Y. S. V.

California, awake ! arise ! 'tis time to sleep no more,
The bright warm sun is even now the mountains peeping o'er ;
Awake ! the night is speeding fast, the clouds have passed away,
Already break the first faint beams of the fast coming day,
And yet, though dark and heavy night has shrouded o'er the mind,
Fair nature in material things has bounteous been and kind.
Thy sleep was in defiance of each rich and saving boon,
A dull and deep Siesta, 'neath the broad full light of noon !
But now the waking hour is nigh, we come to set thee free,
We come as doth the else unfruitful sea,
To speed upon thy bosom, the barks of wealth and peace,
To multiply a thousand fold the California land's increase ;
We come to bring thee blessings rare, which freedom's age hath shed,
Outgushing rich and plenteous as a mighty river head;
We come to scatter then abroad, rich seed, which sown, shall be,
Productive of a happy race, a people wise and free.
Columbia sends her people on a message unto thee,
She would that you were happy, she would that ye were free ;
Receive from her, her people, receive from her, her laws,
Receive from her the spirit of His great and glorious cause,
And when the Future shall mature, what now receives its birth,
When California stands among the mighty powers of earth,
When knowledge, Freedom, and the arts, have bro't forth glorious fruit,
Each rivaling the other in one common grand pursuit.
Then, Californians, pause to think, who brought these blessings rare,
Think who it was first pealed the note of freedom on the air,
And you will learn with heartfelt praise, to bless the happy day,
When freedom took its westward flight to California.

U. S. TRANSPORT SHIP, "LOO CHOO," Feb. 25, 1847.

Andrew J. Cox in the *Napa Register* of October 11, 1879, says: "When Stevenson's Regiment arrived at San Francisco, in March, 1847, there were only four practical printers in California. They were Robert Semple, Edward C. Kemble, Sam. Brannan and P. H. Dunne, who froze his feet in attempting to rescue the Donner party. That the Regiment added 13 more. They were Edward Gilbert, G. C. Hubbard, Walter Murray, James O'Sullivan, David Norris, B. F. Foster, Joshua Rand, William J. Weaver, William Layden, Bela Cushing, Wm. Slade, J. D. Yates and Andrew J. Cox. Kemble and Yates were living in New York in 1879, Norris and Sullivan, Brannan and Cox were living in California 1879–80, and all the rest are dead except, perhaps, Weaver.

RESCUE OF PRISONERS OF WAR AT SAN ANTONIO, L. C.

Captain Steele's Report

La Paz Barracks,
Lower California, March 20, 1848.

Sir: I have the honor to report that, in compliance with your order, I took command of the mounted force destined for an incursion into the interior. On the 15th, and between the hours of 9 and 10 P. M., we started. On examination, I found our whole force consisted of 27 non-commissioned officers and privates, three officers (Surgeon Alexander Perry, Acting Lieut. Scott, B company and myself), Lieut. Halleck, United States Engineers, who kindly volunteered his valuable experience and services, and Messrs. Herman Ehrenberg and Taylor, residents of this place, and three guides, Californians—(aggregate 34). On conferring with the officers, we were unanimous in the conclusion to proceed with all possible speed direct to San Antonio (the headquarters of the enemy), instead of attacking the advance party at the ranche of Noviellas, with the principal object of rescuing the American prisoners of war confined there, and doing all else we could.

We took the route by the ranche of the Tuscalamas. Proceeding cautiously, we passed an outpost of some fifty men, without being observed by them, and reached the top of the mountain, overlooking and eight miles distant from San Antonio, at daylight on the following morning, where we captured one of the "enemy's pickets," and quickening our speed, we descended and passed up the arroyo to the east of the town, and, arranging the men, we charged into the town at full speed. A small party having been previously detailed to secure the persons of the officers of the enemy; the rest were directed against the building occupied as a cuartel for the soldiers; and not finding any there, one of the liberated captives directed my attention to a building on the other side of the arroyo, to the east of the town, distant from the Plaza about 150 yards, and commanding it (to which I afterwards learned the soldiers had been removed but the day previous, thereby deranging all our previous plans of attack), from which, with a small force of the enemy drawn up in front, a brisk fire of musketry opened upon us.

Having first gained our object in rescuing our men, besides taking two of their officers prisoners, I ordered the men to dismount and rally under cover of the church on the east side of the Plaza.

The party sent to secure the officers were unsuccessful in securing the commandant—(he escaped in his night clothes, having just arisen from his bed)—but the second in command, Captain Calderon, and the Adjutant Lieutenant Arsse, were taken, their flag and the private and public papers secured. When a sufficient number of our men had rallied, we sallied out and charged the enemy in position, and drove them in all directions to the adjacent hills, killing three of their number and wounding seven or eight. The rout of their force being complete, which we learned amounted to some fifty men, and being too tired to pursue them, we collected all the arms they abandoned (some thirty), their trumpet, bullet-moulds, etc., destroyed them and left them in the Plaza, as it was impossible to carry them with us.

I have to record the loss of one of our number, Sergeant Thomas M. Hipwood, of B company, who fell dead in the charge, pierced by a bayonet and two balls. "A better and a truer man never fell in his country's service or the performance of his duty; and his loss will ever be lamented by those who knew his worth."

Pantaloons, cravats, hats, horses, saddles, attest the numerous narrow escapes, but none wounded.

Not more than half an hour elapsed before we were on our way back. We halted at a ranche after travelling some ten miles (owing to the accession of our number of men, and but one or two horses, many had to walk that distance), for the first time, to refresh. In two hours we were on our way again, but little recruited in strength. Proceeding slowly, we reached the mountain pass of Trincheras a little before sunset, and were just entering an arroyo, bordered by elevated banks and a thick growth of underbrush, when a fierce fire of musketry opened upon us in front; a dismount and rally in front was but the work of an instant, the men standing fire like veterans. I ordered the advance guard to deploy to the right and left, who drove them from tree to tree and hill to hill, while the main body proceeded slowly, leading their horses, until we had passed the dangerous ground, when we mounted and took a different road, diverging to the right, which would make the distance much further, but the travelling much safer.

There was none wounded on our side. One of the captives, Captain Chalderon, received a severe wound from a rifle ball in the right breast from the fire of the enemy, which did not prevent his riding, however; the horses received several wounds, but not so as to disable them. The loss on the part of the enemy was some five or six killed and wounded. We continued our march, proceeded some three miles further, when our rear guard was attacked; but on firing one musket at them they scampered off, and scarcely a charge ensued. We proceeded cautiously, but our horses were getting now so fatigued that they would lie down, and it was with the greatest perseverance and exertion that we continued advancing, but finally arrived at the barracks on the morning of the 17th at 2 P. M.

Having accomplished the extraordinary distance of 120 miles (the route we took) in less than thirty hours on the same horses, with but little food or refreshment, stopping but once to feed, through the most rocky country and the roughest road that can be travelled, and by men, many of them, totally unused to riding, and without any previous preparation, I cannot express in terms too commendatory the coolness and bravery displayed by the men of my command. Acting Lieutenant Scott, B company, Sergeant Peasley, A company, and Sergeant Denniston, B company, were conspicuous.

To Surgeon Alexander Perry, Lieutenant Halleck, United States Engineers, most sincere thanks are due for their counsel and assistance. And to Mr. Herman Ehrenberg, "my volunteer aid," to say that he fully sustained that reputation for gallantry, coolness and bravery that has been awarded to him on former occasions, is enough.

And to Luz, Morano, and to Juan de Dios Talamantis, our Californian guides, I am greatly indebted; their bravery and fidelity deserve to be duly appreciated.

Respectfully, your obedient servant,

SEYMOUR G. STEELE,

Captain 1st New York Regiment, commanding.

To Lieut. Colonel HENRY S. BURTON,

United States Army, commanding U. S. forces, &c.

[Letter of Col. Stevenson to Col. Mason in behalf of the Men of his Regiment.]

HEAD-QUARTERS SOUTHERN MILITARY DISTRICT, CALIFORNIA,

Los Angeles, California, August 20, 1848.

SIR: I have the honor to acknowledge the receipt of your several communications of the 8th, and proclamation of the 7th instant, together with department orders Nos. 50 and 52, announcing the conclusion of a treaty of peace between the United States and Mexico, and containing instructions for the disbanding of the First Regiment New York Volunteers under my command. Earnestly as all have desired such an event, the very sudden and unexpected termination of our service has surprised us all, and found many a poor fellow, who has served his country faithfully for more than two years, without a dollar beyond the small amount of pay that will be due them at the time of their discharge; and if they pay the few small debts they owe here, they will not have money sufficient to buy a pair of shoes; and I know that many, if not all at this post, possess so high a sense of honor that they would go barefooted rather than leave in debt to any one in the town. Thank God, all here have acted honorably and fairly to the people of the country, and I trust they will do so to the end. Yet, hard as their case is, they do not complain of the want of anything but the means of defence; for when they are disbanded, not ten men will have either a gun or pistol; and I assure you, great fears are entertained, and not without just cause, that they will be wanted, as well for their defence against Indians as against some miserable wretches of the country, who already threaten not only to attack all Americans, but the families of the people of the country who have been friendly to us. My men complain that the Mormons retained their arms, and were allowed transportation to the Salt Lake, for seven months' service, and supplied with twenty rounds of cartridges each, while they, who have served more than two years and travelled thousands of miles on the ocean to come here in the service of their country, are to be discharged without an arm for their defence, or a dollar of commutation; and some of them (the last recruits) had their arms taken from them at Monterey, which, unless you have sent them down in the "Anita," they will, in all human probability, never receive. Soon after I arrived in this country, in a frank conversation with General Kearny on this

very subject, he assured me that my men should be allowed to
retain their arms, as he had no doubt if it had been suggested to
the authorities at home before sailing, it would have been authorized, as they were intended for, and would become, permanent
residents of the country. He said he made the stipulation with
the Mormons, and he felt authorized to make it with me for my
men; and the day he left here for the United States he assured
me that he would leave such instructions with you as would
insure it. A very large number of my men here must remain
until they can raise the means of reaching the upper country, or
go up on foot; which would be a most toilsome and perilous
journey, unarmed as they will be. Under these circumstances, I
have deemed it my duty to present you their most earnest appeal
that you will allow them to retain their arms, and that fifteen
days' rations of such stores as are at the post may be served
out to them on the day they are disbanded. They would
not ask this favor of the Government if they could in any manner
dispose of the land or money scrip. I present this, their petition,
most cheerfully, because I feel that they more than deserve it at
the hands of their Government; for no soldiers, either regulars
or volunteers, have ever surpassed them in correct, honorable
and manly deportment, or in a most faithful and diligent discharge of the duty required of them as soldiers.

I have the honor to be, very respectfully, your obedient
servant,

J. D. STEVENSON,
Colonel 1st New York Regiment,
Commanding Southern Military District.

To Colonel R. B. MASON,
1st United States Dragoons, Governor of California.

[Extract from Letter of Col. Mason to the Adjutant-General of the Army.]

HEAD-QUARTERS, TENTH MILITARY DEPARTMENT,
MONTEREY, CALIFORNIA, June 17, 1848.

* * * * * * *

This regiment, you are aware, had been strung from Sonoma
in the north to San Jose, in Lower California, during their whole

time of service in this quarter. The companies stationed at La Paz (Steele's and Matsell's) held that town for many weeks against four times their numbers; and the very moment they were reinforced by Naglee's company with additional recruits, they took the field under the command of Lieutenant Colonel Burton, routed the enemy, completely dispersed them, and restored peace to the peninsula. Colonel Burton speaks highly of the courage and coolness of his men and officers under fire; and I refer you to his report for individual acts of gallantry. Lieutenant Colonel Burton, throughout his whole conduct whilst in command of the forces in Lower California, completely executed his instructions, which were based upon the orders from the War Department; and as his reports and copies of his instructions are already in your office, I need only add my present approval of his conduct. He is now on duty at this place, in command of his company F, 3d Artillery.

Colonel J. D. Stevenson, since April, 1847, has been in command of the district of country embracing Santa Barbara, Los Angeles, and San Diego, has by energy and good management, maintained most excellent discipline amongst his men, and has preserved harmony amongst the population of that district, which is composed mostly of the native Californians. This required peculiar tact and firmness—qualities possessed by him in a peculiar degree. I will warrant that at no previous time in that district were life and property so secure, the magistrates of the country so effectually supported, and industry so encouraged, as during the past two years; one common cry of regret arose at the order for their disbandment; the little petty causes of complaint were forgotten in the remembrance of the more substantial advantages they had enjoyed under the protection of the military. Subalterns and men are entitled to share with their commander the honor due for this creditable state of feeling on the part of a people nominally conquered. That part of California lying on the bay of San Francisco has been under the command of the Major of this regiment, James A. Hardie, who has effectually aided the civil authorities, dispelled the fears of the threatened Indian incursions, and guarded the heavy depot at San Francisco— duties which were performed to the best advantage with the limited force at his command. His officers and men were generally attentive to their duties, and anxious to serve the United States.

* * * * * * *

R. B. MASON,
Colonel 1st Dragoons, Commanding.

To Brig. Gen. R. JONES.
Adjutant General, U.S. Army, Washington, D.C.

[Extract from letter of Lieut. Sherman to Lieut. Colonel Burton.]

HEAD-QUARTERS TENTH MILITARY DEPARTMENT,
MONTEREY, CALIFORNIA, June 17th, 1848.

* * * * * * *

I take great pleasure in communicating to you Colonel Mason's great satisfaction at hearing of your dispersing the enemy's forces at Todos Santos, and of the previous rescue of the American prisoners at San Antonio, by the party under the immediate command of Captain Steele, First New York Volunteers. These operations were alike creditable in their conception and execution.

Colonel Mason wishes you to convey to the officers and men under your command his thanks for their gallantry and good conduct displayed on those occasions.

I have the honor to be, very respectfully, your obedient servant.

W. T. SHERMAN,
1st Lieut. 3d Artillery, A. A. A. General.

To Lieutenant Colonel H. S. BURTON,
Commanding in Lower California.

[Extract from a letter written by General Nelson Taylor, of South Norwalk, Conn. Many of the facts related in the letter of General Taylor having already appeared in other parts of this work, are omitted here.]

SOUTH NORWALK, CONN., February 1st, 1882.

FRIEND CLARK—In response to your request, asking for information in relation to our old regiment, or more particularly, that portion of the command with which I served, has been received, and I will endeavor to comply with your wishes, notwithstanding thirty-five years have nearly elapsed since our discharge from the service on the Pacific coast, and only memory to rely upon.

* * * * * * *

During the summer of 1848 an order was received by Col. R. B. Mason, commanding Tenth Military Department, from the War Department, directing that Col. Stevenson's regiment should be designated thereafter the " First Regiment New York Volunteers," instead of the *Seventh*, as heretofore. This fact was never generally known outside of California, and the regiment, subsequently organized and commanded by Colonel Ward B. Burnett, which served in Mexico, has always been known as the First Regiment New York Volunteers, when it should have been designated as the *Second*, and was so designated in an official order issued by the War Department in 1847. There were but two regiments organized in the State of New York during the Mexican war, ours being the *First*.

On the night of December 7th, 1847, a casualty occurred at Los Angeles which cast a gloom over the entire garrison, and so impressed the commander, that its influence seemed to be felt to the end of the organization. An old lady called on the Colonel that afternoon, and informed him that a large body of Californians had organized, and intended to attempt the re-taking of the city that night. Being the officer of the day, I was summoned to the Colonel's quarters and informed of the substance of the lady's story, and, as a consequence, special vigilance was enjoined on the officer of the guard and each sentry on post. At midnight I visited the guard, as also each sentry on post, and finding everything quiet, and believing this story to be as groundless as a hundred other similar ones which had preceded it, I went to my quarters, and in about twenty minutes, certainly not more than half an hour afterwards, I was brought suddenly to my feet by the report of a terrible explosion. Believing that an attack had actually been made, the whole command were promptly got under arms at the barracks; and after waiting a reasonable time, and hearing nothing further, I proceeded to the guard-house, situated on a side hill overlooking the city, and never will the sad spectacle which presented itself to my view, as I approached its precincts, be forgotten. The night was quite dark, and before I could fairly see what had occurred, I was startled with the sound of voices giving expression to the most intense suffering, and, on approaching nearer, I found a portion of the guard-house blown down; one or two men were lying dead on the ground; a number slightly, a number seriously, and two or three mortally injured, and the remainder in the greatest confusion.

On an investigation it was ascertained that private Earl, of Company E, on post a short distance from the guard-house, challenged a horseman, who made a response, but continued to ride towards the sentry, when the challenge was repeated with no better success, and, thinking an attempt was being made to ride him down, Earl fired his musket and retreated towards the guard-house. The report of the gun having been heard at the guard-house, the guard was promptly turned out and formed, when a soldier of Company G lighted a port fire to use on a piece of artillery stationed at the guard-house, if the emergency of the case demanded. The officer of the guard retained the men under arms until he satisfied himself that Earl's horseman was an imaginary one, or that he had been frightened away by the shot from Earl's musket, when he ordered the ranks broken, and directed the man with the port fire to extinguish and return it to the arm chest from whence it had been taken. The arm chest was kept in the room of the officer of the guard, and was well filled with amunition. The man, not understanding the almost impossibility of extinguishing a lighted port fire without cutting off the lighted end, stamped it until it was black, and, as he doubtless thought, extinguished the fire, when he threw it back into the chest, and closed the lid. In a very few minutes the hidden spark rekindled, fired and exploded the amunition, causing the painful and distressing scene which ensued. The poor fellow, who had so unwittingly caused the sad casualty, was not found until the next day; he had paid the full penalty of his ignorance or carelessness, or both. The loss in men fell on Company G of our regiment, and Company C, First U S. Dragoons. Three or four of Company E were injured, and they but slightly.

* * * * * * *

In closing this brief sketch of my recollection of that portion of the regiment with which I served, it is my desire to pay a well merited tribute to a worthy officer, that was the Colonel of the regiment, Jonathan D. Stevenson.

Doubtless, with the experience he now has, if called upon to organize and command another regiment he would leave undone many things which he felt called upon to do, and do many others which he left undone. Such, I believe to be the feeling of most men having had the experience of organizing and commanding regiments; but upon a careful review of his colonelcy, I entertain the opinion that few volunteer officers who served during the Mexican war, acquitted themselves with more advantage to the Government, or greater credit to themselves.

It is true he performed no brilliant military achievement in the field, where honor is sought at the cannon's mouth; his lines happened to fall in more pleasant places; yet, if occasion had called for it, and opportunity offered, there is no doubt but that his field services would have been as distinguished and creditable as was his civil administration satisfactory to the citizens of his military district. To his superior administrative and executive ability is due, in my humble opinion, the peace and good order that prevailed so uninterruptedly throughout the lower portion of Upper California after he assumed the command of that district.

His intercourse with those who were brought in contact with him officially or otherwise, was ever characterized with the easy and agreeable courtesy which betokens a well-bred gentleman, and which deservedly made him popular, both with the soldiers of his command and the citizens of his military district.

It is many years since it was my good pleasure to meet the Colonel, whom, I learn, still remains a citizen of the Golden State, and which he has never left for a single day, since he first landed on its shores in command of our regiment. Let him reside where he may, he has my best wishes for all the worldly prosperity and mental contentment which can fall to the lot of man.

Truly yours, NELSON TAYLOR,
Formerly Captain Co. E.

The military forces in Cal. in April, 1847, were about as folows:

One Company 1st U. S. Dragoons,	88 men.
One Company 3d U. S. Artillery,	107 men.
Ten Companies N. Y. Volunteers.	550 men.
Five Companies Mormon Battalion.	314 men.
Total,	1,059

MEXICAN CALIFORNIA.

The following chapter from a work recently published by Major Bell, entitled "Reminiscences of a Ranger," gives to those who are unfamiliar with California prior to its acquisition by the Americans, a truthful account of the simple, pastoral life of its inhabitants. Major Bell says:

"If I am correct, before the coming of the gringo in '46, the Mexican province of California contained a population of 30,000, not counting the Indians. This population extended along the coast from San Diego to Sonoma, a distance of say 600 miles. There being only a few towns, San Diego being first, then Los Angeles, Santa Barbara, San Luis, Obispo, Monterey, Santa Cruz, San Jose, Yerba Buena, and last of all, going north, Sonoma. Los Angeles was the largest, containing a population of about 2,000. Next came Santa Barbara and Monterey, mere villages. Now, it is quite easy for the reader to perceive that the major part of the population dwelt on the ranchos. These ranchos ranged in size from one to eleven leagues—that is, in round numbers, from five thousand to fifty thousand acres. The owner of each rancho possessed from one thousand to ten thousand head of horned cattle, and from one or two hundred to three or four thousand head of horses, broken and bronco. The country, even when the value of a bullock was his hide, tallow and horns, was prosperous, and money plenty. The rancheros dressed well, were well housed, and had an abundance of store—home produce and foreign importation.

"The hospitality of the California ranchero was a proverb. A person, though he may have been a stranger to the country born, could start from San Diego and journey to Sonoma without it costing him a dollar, and be furnished with a fresh horse at every rancho, leaving instead the one of the previous day's ride. Such a thing as charging a traveler for what he received would have been considered an act of excessive meanness. The social intercourse and amusements of these isolated people were in keeping with their situation. Religious fiestas were celebrated at the Pueblos and Missions with great pomp and ceremony, and afforded a pleasant recreation and relief from the monotony of ranch life. When the daughter of a ranchero married, the family either gave a grand fiesta at the rancho or a baile at the Pueblo or

Mission, to which the whole country were invited, except the lower classes, and to which the people came sometimes a distance of forty leagues or more, families traveling in their elaborately fixed up carretas, and the beaux transporting the belles before them on their elegant saddles, the beau occupying a seat on the croup, with his bridle arm resting on the shoulder of his fair passenger, or encircling her slender waist. While the families were absent on these social expeditions nothing would go amiss on the ranchos. The major-domo and the Indian vaqueros would look out for the herds as though the patron were present; the grass would grow and the cattle would thrive and multiply. These marriage feasts would be of three or four days' duration. Dancing at night and horse racing during the day, and generally winding up with bull-fighting. The religious feasts, celebrated at the churches, were brilliant, pompous, expensive and imposing, the most important of which were the feast of the Holy Week, Corpus Christi and St. John's Day, the latter being devoted to cock-fighting and kindred amusements, one of which was to take a live cock, and, after plucking the feathers from and thoroughly greasing his neck, his body would be buried in the middle of the street or road, the greased neck alone being exposed above the ground. Now, the game was to dash past the buried cock at full speed on horseback, and lean over and seize the neck and pull the cock from the ground—a most difficult performance. The feast of Corpus Christi was one of peculiar religious observance —one of processions, parades and displays. The feast of the Holy Week always ended with a tragedy on the Saturday of Glory, in the annual execution of that eminent traitor, Judas Iscariot, which was done by first erecting a gibbet; then an effigy of Judas was brought forth from an imaginary prison, mounted on a cart, with the arms pinioned, and being guarded by a file of soldiers, was drawn around the plaza and principal streets, followed by the excited crowd, hooted at, insulted and pelted by the boys and others, and finally, in a most dilapidated and disgraceful condition, was halted in front of the gibbet. Now, an orator from the crowd comes forward and delivers a solemn lecture to Judas, and gives him fits, makes his bow and retires, and is succeeded by another orator, who gives Judas another berating, and accuses him of crimes so contemptible and manifold that, as an impartial judge, one feels constrained to take sides with the old sinner, and declare one's utter disbelief in those divers and many crimes charged against him—such, for instance, as robbing hen-roosts, of stealing old clothes, of dealing cards unfairly in the national game of monte, of being a cheat, a vagabond, Jew, and worst of all, a gringo. Poor old Judas stands this without a word of denial, and by standing mute is deemed to have pleaded guilty, is taken from the cart, raised to and bound on the gibbet. The crowd again commence to insult and pelt him, all of which old Judas endures without a word of remonstrance; stands like a martyr. The tragedy is about to end as the shades of eve fall upon the scene.

Now we hear the strains of martial music, the solemn tap of the drum, and the heavy tramp of military feet, as a platoon of infantry file into line and halt in front of the doomed traitor. Now the judgment of the court is read and the death warrant recited, and Judas is given an opportunity to speak for himself, but remains as mute as a dead mutton, which is taken as an acknowledgement that the judgment is just, and that he ought to die. Now the military commander orders his men to "load! shoulder arms! ready! aim! fire!" and poor Judas, for the eighteen hundredth time or more suffers a public execution. The volley riddles him. Then "load and fire at will," and the soldiers take huge delight in firing at Judas until there is not a piece of him left large enough for a cigar wrapper. In the meantime the band plays, the crowd yell and hoot in triumphant glee, and Judas is sent to the devil until Saturday the year coming, when he is again disposed of in the same way.

After the gringo nation had nailed its flag to the mast in this angel land, the ceremonies attending the annual execution of Judas became less inspiring and satisfactory, because of there being no military to blow the old traitor into the next year.

Some of the great ranchos of the country were baronial in their extent and surroundings. Their proprietors being great dignitaries, maintaining large numbers of vassals—for such really they were—mostly Indians, who, under Mexican major-domos, did all of the labor for the ranch. The chief major-domo, under the immediate direction of the patron, had entire supervision of the business; then there was the major-domo de la casa, or steward; the major-domo del campo had charge of the vaqueros, or mounted herders in the field; the major-domo de las caponeras had full control of the gentle horses; the major-domo de las mandas was in charge of thousands of wild mares and their foals, and attended to the branding of colts, others to the marking and branding of cattle. There were hair-rope and halter makers, others who made cinches or broad hair girths, makers of raw hide riatas, the curers of hides, the triers out of tallow, the hewers of wood and the carreta men, all of whom amounted to hundreds of people dependent upon the ranchero or lord of the manor. At morn you hear the clatter of horses' feet and the jingling of spurs, as the mounted men, hat in hand, report for duty to the major-domo-in-chief, and then, in detachments, dash off at a full gallop in all directions to their respective duties. By this time coffee is served in the dining-hall, and the patron, members of his household, and guests take their morning cup. At nine or ten o'clock the vaqueros begin to return from the field, and a herd of gentle horses are driven into the corral, fresh ones are caught, and those of the day before are turned loose, may be not to be used again for a week; the fresh ones are saddled, and then the under major-domos report to the chief, who in turn, hat in hand, reports to the patron, and then the whole ranch, goes to breakfast, which being disposed of, the duties of the day are resumed.

[The following extract, taken from the work entitled "The Natural Wealth of California," by Titus Fey Cronise, published at San Francisco in 1868, twenty years subsequent to the disbandment of the regiment, thus speaks of the character established in later years by the former members of Col. Stevenson's regiment. It says:]

"Another valuable accession to the early settlers was made by the arrival of Colonel Stevenson's Regiment of California volunteers, consisting of nearly one thousand rank and file, in anticipation of movements which were subsequently developed. In 1846 President Polk authorized Colonel J. D. Stevenson to raise a regiment of infantry volunteers in New York, for the purpose of protecting the interests of the United States on the Pacific coast. The men comprising this regiment were selected particularly with the object of their becoming settlers in the country; many of them have become permanent and honored citizens of the State. In its ranks, as privates, were sons of senators and representatives in Congress, lawyers, doctors, editors, printers, and representatives of nearly every trade, who were all permitted to bring tools and material for carrying on their respective occupations—being in striking contrast to the soldiers sent here by the Mexican Government, who were generally the worst convicts from the jails, and such refractory, turbulent characters as it was most desirable to get rid of.

The California regiment left New York on the 26th of October* 1846, on board the ships, "Thomas H. Perkins," "Loo Choo," and "Susan Drew." The first division, under command of Colonel Stevenson, on board the "Thomas H. Perkins," arrived at San Francisco March 6th, 1847. The regiment was mustered out of service in the summer of 1848. Nearly three hundred of its members were alive, in California, in July, 1867. Among its commissioned officers were Captain Folsom, Lieutenant Harrison and Captain Taylor, whose names are connected with streets formed on land they acquired. Captains H. M. Naglee and J. B. Frisbie held prominent positions in the history of the State. W. E. Shannon, the delegate from Sacramento to the State Constitutional Convention, was Captain of Company I of this regiment. *The volunteer service of the United States has been honored by the exemplary conduct of the members of Col. Stevenson's regiment."*

The following account of the explosion of the magazine at Los Angeles, Cal., is furnished by Col. John McH. Hollinsworth, from a journal kept by him while on duty at that post:

"DECEMBER 9TH, 1847.

"The magazine has blown up and killed some of our brave fellows. We were informed by native Californians, friendly to our cause, that we should be attacked last night. Accordingly, every preparation was made to receive the enemy. When night came on I felt very anxious, and, though not on duty, and no responsibility resting upon me, yet I could not sleep. At midnight I put on my side arms, and, in company with Captain Stevenson, patroled the town. We met Sergeant Travers of the guard, one of my company, going around with a patrol, to see if all was right. He halted us, and, upon recognizing who

---

* The author is in error—the month was September. He also omits mention of the subsequent arrivals of ships "Brutus," "Isabella," and "Sweden," with detachments of the regiment.

we were, made the customary salute. I had not long returned to our quarters, when we heard the report of a musket from the furthermost outpost of the redoubt. Another report followed in rapid succession, and then a bright blaze lit up the heavens, followed by a deafening roar, which seemed to come from the centre of our guard. Meanwhile we heard the drum rolling, and horses moving around our quarters. We armed ourselves, and passed out the back way, concluding we were surrounded, and must fight our way out. I opened the gate. No one was there; but I passed as rapidly and silently as I could along the shadow of the wall, to reach my company, for, as no one doubted but that the long expected attack had come. Horsemen were riding up and down the street in every direction. I looked back to see if anyone was following, and found my Captain (Stevenson) next to me, with his broad, white belt passed across his shoulder and breast. I advised him to take it off instantly, unless he wished to be a target for the enemy's bullets. Upon reaching the company it pressed forward; we were at the same moment joined by Captain Nelson Taylor and his men, and together we ran up the hill. All was still and dark when we set off, and we asked each other, 'Had the guard been overpowered? or had the ground been undermined and all blown into the air?' As we neared the scene of action, a spectacle presented itself which I hope never again to witness. The magazine had been opened to man the battery, when a spark from a port fire had fallen into it, through the carelessness of one of the men. The groans and shrieks of the wounded and dying, the shouting of the officers to the men, and the incessant roll of the drum, while everything was enveloped in a dense cloud of smoke, formed a terrible scene of confusion. I heard the Colonel calling for me to take command of a party of soldiers who had already dug seven bodies out of the ruins. I hastily collected some men to convey the injured to the hospital. Three of them were burnt to a crisp, three burnt black, but with life still left, calling upon God to give them back their eyesight, which was gone forever It was thought at the time that at least twenty men were killed. All were knocked down who were near, though many were unharmed by it. The guard-chair, where I had so often sat, was shattered into a thousand atoms. The Lieutenant, although not in the chair at the time, was thrown some distance, but picked up unhurt. I saw a dragoon dug out from under the wall of the guard-house. He lived but a few minutes. I heard one of the poor fellows calling for Lieut. H.; I went to him directly, and, though burnt black, I instantly recognized the poor Sergeant (Travers) I had met but an hour before. He said: 'Lieutenant, tell me, as a man, can I live until morning?' I told him I hoped to see him get well. One of the men said: 'The iron hinge of the magazine chest is driven into his body.' I said, 'Hush; do not alarm him.' The poor man said: 'Lieutenant, you cannot deceive me; I am mortally wounded; I have lost my leg; my eyes are gone, all is dark to me. Oh, that my poor mother were here to pray for me!' He then said: 'Doctor, I am sleepy; if I go to sleep will I wake again?' The doctor said, 'It is doubtful.' Travers then said: 'Do not frighten my wife; tell her to be a good girl; I die content.'"·

[From the *Daily Examiner* (San Francisco), March 27th, 1872.

TWENTY-FIFTH ANNIVERSARY.

STEVENSON'S REGIMENT REUNITED.

The Twenty-fifth Anniversary of the landing of that famous body of pioneers, Stevenson's Regiment, was celebrated last evening at Martin's Restaurant. The following survivors were present: Colonel Jonathan D. Stevenson. Co. A—Frederick L. Post, John Flood, Joseph McDonough, James O'Sullivan, Edward Barthrop, J. P. Hawkins. Co. B—James E. Nuttman, Patrick Lynch, James W. Melvin, Lieut. Thomas E. Ketchum. Co. C—Adolphus G. Russ, A. J. Cox, James G. Dow. Co. D—William S. Johnson, James Sirey, Frank P. Anderson, Charles Rosseau. Co. E—Castor Briggs, Major John M. O'Neill, Ezekiel Bullock, Henry J. Wolgemuth. Co. F—Sergeant James Queen, Emil A. Engelberg, Peter Sesser. Co. G—James H. Adams, John Kleinschroth, Robert Wilson, Frederick Coyan. Co. H—Captain John B. Frisbie, Sergeant Eleazar Frisbie, George N. Cornwell, Alfred Guthrie. Co. I—George J. Graff. Co. K—None. Dr. William C. Parker, Surgeon; James C. L. Wadsworth, Clerk to Sutler; John Q. Adams, "at Large."

Letters were received from a number of absentees, expressing their regret at being unable to attend the re-union. The tables were well supplied, the wines excellent, and at a late hour the toasts came in and were responded to most happily.

The Third toast, "The Army and Navy," was drank amid great enthusiasm. The band played the "Red, White and Blue."

General Schofield, U. S. Army, commanding Department of the Pacific, responded. He said it afforded him great pleasure to meet the members of the pioneer regiment of California, and congratulate them upon their re-union. I am surprised, said he, to see so many of the gallant band together, after a lapse of twenty-five years, and so goodly a number of young men, too. I scarcely believe there is, among you, an older man than I am, and I am not yet twenty-five years in the service. It shows the character of our early soldiers, that they were men of vigor, of good habits and of good character. I assure you it gives me pleasure to witness the re-union of those who are of our early pioneers, and who have done so much to develop our country. I wish you many long years of prosperity. (Cheers.)

"The Press" was the fifth regular toast. It was responded to by that venerable pioneer, Hon. Philip A. Roach, in a pertinent and happy speech. He returned thanks for the honor conferred, and said that the subject could be better handled by younger members of the press present. He said, with your regiment, and as one of its number, a member of the press came to our shores, who established a free, fearless and independent paper in this city, and who was not afraid to speak out boldly. When it was dangerous to give utterance to his sentiments, he stood up for the people's rights, and by his fearless and brilliant character built up a paper of influence, talent and ability in this city—the *Alta*. This gentleman's name, you well know, is Edward Gilbert, who laid down his life for what he believed were the principles of liberty we now enjoy and for the liberty of the press. His portrait very properly hangs in the Council Chamber of the city. He lost his life in maintaining his idea of what was right and combatting what was wrong.

Mr. Roach's address was warmly received. A brother of Mr. Roach was a lieutenant in the regiment.

The Volunteer toasts were happily proposed, and their responses in every instance full of kindly sentiment and good fellowship. At a late hour the re-union broke up.

1847—RE-UNION AT NEW YORK—1874.

The twenty-seventh anniversary of the landing of Stevenson's Regiment in California was celebrated by a dinner at the Sturtevant House on the evening of the 26th of March, 1874.

The following survivors were present: Surgeon Alex. Perry, Capt. James M. Turner, Lieut. Jeremiah Sherwood, James E. Nuttman, Russell Myers, William H. Christian, George M. Leonard, William H. Rogers, Jacob J. Schoonmaker, Francis D. Clark and John Taylor.

Letters of regret were read from the following comrades: Major-General James A. Hardie, U. S. A., Gen. Nelson Taylor, Gen. Francis J. Lippitt, John Wolf, Esq. and Hon. Sherman O. Houghton, M. C.

Among the many old Californians present were, Hon. C. K. Garrison, ex-Mayor of San Francisco, Gen. Thomas B. Van Buren, Gen. H. G. Gilson, U. S. A., James Stark, Esq. (the pioneer actor), and Major William W. Leland, (founder of the *Pacific News* at San Francisco in 1849).

The *New York Herald*, in its issue of August 10, 1846, contains an engraving entitled "The Encampment of the California Regiment on Governor's Island," showing the regiment on parade, and its issue of September 6 has another entitled " Presentation of Bibles to the New York Legion or California Regiment," on Governor's Island, by Rev. Dr. McVicar.

[From the *Albany Argus*, August 1st, 1846.]

Yesterday Governor Wright issued commissions to the field officers of the Seventh Regiment of U. S. Volunteers from the State of New York, viz.: Jonathan D. Stevenson, Colonel; Henry S. Burton, Lieutenant-Colonel; James A. Hardie, Major.

MUSTERED OUT IN 1873.

To Lieutenant Jeremiah Sherwood of Company G, the honor belongs of having been the last officer holding a commission in a volunteer regiment enrolled for service during the Mexican war, to be mustered out of the service of the United States. Lieut. S., at the date of the discharge of Company G, at Los Angeles, Cal., September 18th, 1848, was absent upon detached service under Lieut. George Stoneman, U. S. Dragoons. Upon the news of the discharge of a portion of Stevenson's Regiment reaching Lieut. Stoneman, who was then in the neighborhood of San Francisco, he gave Lieut. Sherwood an indefinite furlough. Twenty-five years subsequent Lieut. Sherwood recalled this fact that he was still in the United States service; he addressed several communications to the War Department on the subject, and after he had assured the Department that no claim for pay would be made upon the Government, was the least attention given to the communications. Then the Adjutant-General of the Army issued an order to Gen. Winfield S. Hancock, U. S. A., commanding the Military Division of the Atlantic, with Headquarters at New York, directing that officer to have Lieut. Sherwood properly mustered out of the service of the United States; and upon the muster-out roll of Company G, the War Department has appended opposite to the name of Lieut. S., the following in *red* ink: "A. G. O. Discharge furnished to date from September 18th, 1848, per Special Order 93, par. 3, Headquarters Military Division of the Atlantic, series of 1873." The remarks made by Capt. Smith, U. S. Dragoons, who mustered out the company at Los Angeles, opposite the name of Lieut. Sherwood being: "Absent on detached service by Special Order No. 40, Headquarters Southern Military District, Los Angeles."

CONCLUSION.

COMRADES:

This publication was delayed some four months to enable additional facts regarding surviving, as also deceased comrades to be obtained, thereby affording the opportunity of recording herein information that must otherwise have been omitted. Every effort was used to learn who of those who are recorded under "whereabouts unknown," were living or deceased. In some instances the result was favorable. Undoubtedly many others will be accounted for after this record refreshes the memory, by recalling familiar names to those who were their associates in the regiment, or afterwards identified with them in civil life.

Some twenty names have been received who are reported to have been members of the regiment, but as the official rolls of the respective companies fail to substantiate the fact, it is evident that some mistake has been made, in nearly every instance they are reported as *deceased*.

Want of space has prevented the publication herein of communications written by our comrades, Captain Seymour G. Steele, Lieutenant John C. Bonnycastle, John B. Parvin, William H. Rogers and William H. Christain, containing interesting reminiscences relating to the old regiment.

The printing, binding and distribution by mail of four hundred copies of this little volume necessitates an expense of over three hundred and fifty dollars, it being intended for private distribution among comrades, and through them to personal friends and relatives (excepting those copies which will be forwarded to historical and other societies in the Empire and the Golden State for preservation), the funds for the liquidation of this expense is derived solely from the voluntary contributions of survivors of the old regiment, the small number of copies required greatly increased the cost of each book; and, in response to my appeal for funds to defray this expense, it affords me pleasure to acknowledge the receipt of one half of the amount required from the following comrades :

Colonel JONATHAN D. STEVENSON.
Lieutenant J. C. BONNYCASTLE, Adjutant.

Co. A.

WILLIAM H. ROGERS.
ANDREW J. MOORE.
RUSSELL MYERS.
WILLIAM H. WILLIAMS.
JOHN W. THOMAS.
WILLIAM WOOLEY.
JOHN B. PARVIN.
THEODORE R. SAUNDERS.
MOSES W. PERRY.

Co. B.

Lieut. THOMAS E. KETCHUM.
JAMES E. NUTTMAN.
CHARLES H. THURSTON.
CHARLES HEINRICH.
SAMUEL CATTS.

Co. D.

WILLIAM S. JOHNSON.
JAMES M. HARRON.
JOHN WOLFE.
GEORGE A. CORGAN.
FRANCIS D. CLARK.

Co. E.

Capt. NELSON TAYLOR.
JOHN M. O'NEIL.
JOHN H. WELSH.
GEORGE CANFIELD.

Co. F.

Capt. FRANCIS J. LIPPITT.
CHAS. C. E. RUSS.
JAMES LYNCH.
AUGUST E. ENGELBERG.
AMISON WHITAKER.

Co. G.

Lieut. JEREMIAH SHERWOOD.
" J. McH. HOLLINGSWORTH.
ROBERT WILSON.
E. D. SHIRLAND.
THOMAS NISBITT.

Co. H.

Capt. JOHN B. FRISBIE.
SQUIRE G. MERRILL.
GEORGE VAN VECHTEN.
JAMES H. LAPPEUS.

Co. I.

JOSEPH EVANS.
EUGENE GUIBAL.

The Legislature of the State of New York has recently passed an act appropriating the sum of fifty thousand dollars for the purpose of granting to each survivor of the First Regiment of New York Volunteers, which served in the Mexican war, the sum of twelve dollars per month for a period of two years. The act only awaits at this date, (June 1st, 1882,) the signature of the Governor to become a law. At the first glance it would be supposed that this allowance was for the survivors of the regiment under Colonel Jonathan D. Stevenson. Such is not the fact.

Disputes having arisen, and more or less confusion still existing in the minds of many, with reference to the proper designation of our regiment, it seems not inappropriate to here state a few facts, giving a clear and better understanding of the matter.

At the outbreak of the Mexican war an attempt was made to organize *six* regiments in the State of New York, and while these were in the course of completion the War Department issued authority to Colonel Jonathan D. Stevenson to organize a regiment in the State of New York for service in California, and naturally, this latter regiment took the designation of "Seventh Regiment New York Volunteers," under which title it was mustered into the service, and took its departure for its field of duty. The effort to organize the six regiments, above referred to, was, subsequent to the sailing of the regiment under Col. Stevenson for California, abandoned, owing to the fact that the War Department declined to accept only one other regiment from the State of New York for duty in Mexico. Out of these six partly organized regiments, owing to a compromise made between several of the would-be colonels, was formed the regiment which served in Mexico under the command of Colonel Ward B. Burnett, which was the *second* and last New York regiment organized and mustered into the service of the United States during the Mexican war. Colonel Stevenson's regiment having been mustered into the service as the *Seventh*, and having sailed for California, the State authorities designated the regiment under Colonel Burnett the *First*.

The War Department subsequently corrected this erroneous designation of New York regiments, by an order directing Col. Stevenson to thereafter designate and muster his regiment as the "First Regiment of New York Volunteers," which order, upon its receipt by Col. Stevenson at Los Angeles, Cal., early in 1848, through Col. R. B. Mason, 1st U. S. Dragoons, commanding in

California was immediately complied with. An order was also issued by the War Department and forwarded to Col. Burnett, through the headquarters of Gen. Winfield Scott, commanding the U. S. Army in Mexico, directing Colonel B. to thereafter designate and muster his regiment as the "Second Regiment of New York Volunteers." Col. Burnett, in an interview with the writer in the Fall of 1873, gave the following as his reason for declining to obey the order:

Col. B. said: "An order was received from Gen. Winfield Scott, commanding the Armies of the United States in Mexico, directing me to discontinue mustering my regiment as the *First*, and returning the rolls for correction. I maintained that by so doing I would invalidate my commission, received from the Governor of the State of New York, by which I was designated Colonel of the First Regiment of New York Volunteers, under which designation it was mustered into the service of the United States, and that only under the authority of the State of New York could the designation of my regiment be changed."

Col. B. was, however, required thereafter to muster his regiment upon the muster rolls as the *Second*. Col. Stevenson, on the contrary, who held his commission under the same authority, never questioned the right of the Government to change the designation of his regiment from that of the *Seventh* to the *First*.

Col. B. still holds to the disputed title, and on all public occasions or parades in the City of New York the survivors of his regiment floats at their head a flag upon which is inscribed: "First Regiment of New York Volunteers, Mexican war—Col. Ward B. Burnett."

Not a member of the regiment under the command of Colonel Jonathan D. Stevenson, from the State of New York, in the Mexican war, would deprive the members of Colonel Ward B. Burnett's regiment of one iota of the glory they so nobly achieved upon many well fought battle fields in the valley of Mexico. To the contrary, the members of Col. Stevenson's regiment are proud of the record gained in Mexico by their brother New York regiment; but the confusion that continually arises through the same designation to both regiments ought not to exist. The members of Col. Stevenson's regiment have never received nor asked for any special favor from the National, or any State Government, while the present is the second instance in which the State of New York has granted to the members of the regiment under Col. Burnett a gratuity; and yet the survivors of Col. Stevenson's regiment are none the less soldiers of the Empire State who went forth under her banner for service in the Mexican war.

The following letter, received from the War Department, is evidence that Col. Stevenson's regiment is recognized in that office as the *First*:

WAR DEPARTMENT, ADJUTANT GENERAL'S OFFICE,
WASHINGTON, November 18, 1881.

FRANCIS D. CLARK, ESQ.,
    38 Cortlandt street, New York City.

SIR—In reply to your several letters, addressed to the Secretary of War, the General of the Army, and to General Lippitt, of the Department of Justice, I respectfully transmit herewith skeleton copies of the muster out rolls of the First Regiment of New York Volunteers, Mexican War.

Very respectfully, your obedient servant,

H. C. CORBIN,
Asst. Adjutant General.

Letters having been received from comrades who are now residents of the Atlantic States expressing a wish that arrangements might be effected for a re-union, in the near future, of survivors of the old command at New York. The suggestions were submitted to comrades residing in the City of New York, and met with a favorable response, accordingly a call will be issued inviting those comrades who can possibly attend to assemble in the City of New York, on Tuesday, the 26th day of September next, the Thirty-sixth Anniversary of the sailing of the regiment from this port bound for California, upon which occasion a dinner will be given by the New York survivors to their visiting comrades from neighboring cities. The suggestion is therefore made that our surviving comrades at San Francisco might also inaugurate a movement for a re-union upon the same date in that city—among whom they have our old and venerable colonel, to whom such a meeting would without doubt prove of the greatest possible pleasure. Let all, therefore, who possibly can, make the 26th day of September next a joyous day for the survivors of the old regiment. A few years hence our roll will undoubtedly be greatly diminished.

I am persuaded to recall these words, "with this publication I bring my labors to a close," which appear in my introductory remarks, feeling that the labor of the past eleven years should not close until at least *one more effort* was made to learn who of those under "Whereabouts unknown" are living or deceased, and, within a few months after this little waif reaches our comrades, information ought to be received that will unravel the mystery surrounding those names, all are therefore asked to furnish such facts in relation thereto as a refreshed memory will permit, which facts will be compiled in a circular sheet and forwarded to comrades, thereby forming an appendix to the present issue. Let the information that is furnished be *positive*.

To those comrades from whom letters of encouragement have been received within the past few months, expressive of their thanks and satisfaction at the effort being made through my humble labors to once more re-unite old acquaintances, I can only reiterate, the labor was one of pleasure and love. The action of those comrades whose names appear on folio 90 is conclusive that those labors are appreciated. What greater reward than those kindly expressions for such humble efforts could be asked for a self-imposed duty? With the hope that the result will contribute an hour of pleasant reflection to those who were my associates on the Pacific Coast in years ante-dating "The days of old, the days of gold, the days of '49."

    Fraternally yours,

            FRANCIS D. CLARK.

No. 38 Cortlandt Street,
NEW YORK, June 1st, 1882.

APPENDIX.

CONTAINING ADDITIONAL **NAMES** OF SURVIVORS REPORTED SINCE THE ISSUE OF THE VOLUME, **JUNE** 1ST, 1882; DEATHS OF COMRADES DURING **THE PAST THIRTEEN MONTHS;** FURTHER INFORMATION RELATIVE TO DEATHS REGISTERED IN THE VOLUME, AND NAMES REPORTED *WHICH DO NOT APPEAR* ON THE OFFICIAL ROLLS OF THE REGIMENT.

ALSO,

NAMES OF THE CONTRIBUTORS **TO** THE PUBLICATION **FUND,** EXTRACTS FROM LETTERS RECEIVED FROM COMRADES AND OTHERS IN COMMENDATION OF "THE LITTLE VOLUME,"

ETC., ETC., ETC.

New York, August 1st, 1883.

COMRADES:

With the few pages comprising the Appendix to this little volume, the labor of years in the interest of our old regiment and its survivors, are brought to a close. Those of you who have aided in this work, either through information furnished or money contributed, have the satisfaction of feeling that the survivors of the regiment have been benefited thereby, for through that assistance the little volume has been published, and placed in the hands of every known survivor. My own labor and exertions have been a pleasure, and I feel grateful for the expressions of satisfaction and friendliness conveyed in over *one hundred letters* received from members of the old regiment. If a line has crept into the little book calculated to give offense to any one of my comrades, it was through oversight on my part. Certainly, I would not at this late day wound the feelings of any member of the old command.

In bringing my labors to a close, permit me to express the hope that our surviving comrades may not again become so estranged from each other as I found them in 1870, when the task was assumed of searching out their whereabouts; for certainly, at that date, few of us were aware of the existence or place of residence of ten other comrades. Let us ever bear in remembrance the pleasant and happy reminiscences of the days we passed in the old organization, the majority of us being at that time mere youths. At this date, with a few individual exceptions, we remember each other only as we appeared in early life. May we cherish our early friendship, and always honor the name of our respected and venerable Colonel, whose life God still spares, and who, although now past the allotted four-score, is still in the enjoyment of vigorous health, and in the pursuit of his daily labors as an honored servant of the Government, and a creditable citizen of California.

The organization of our survivors into a society is impracticable, from the fact that our places of abode are so far apart. Yet where there are a sufficient number in any one locality, they can at least form themselves into a brotherhood, and once each year spread their board with *Tortillas*, *Frijoles* and *Carni-Seco*, and pass a few hours in social converse.

Though our Government still neglects its duty to the aged and infirm "Veterans of the Mexican War,"—men, who in the fulfilment of their contract rendered faithful and honorable service in that which gave honor, wealth and territory to the country—let us hope that their claims may yet be favorably considered by Congress, and the pension which they have so long appealed for be granted. Of our regiment, perhaps, there is a less number of survivors in need of this aid than there is of any other in the service during that war, yet even among our own comrades there are those who would be greatly benefited by such help from the Government in their declining years.

The present is, in all probability, the last attempt I shall make to issue a printed list of the survivors of our old regiment; still, it is not my purpose to discontinue the record of deaths as they may occur, if apprised thereof. Having completed an *almost* accurate record of the living, I ask to be informed of any change that may occur among our members by death or otherwise.

Fraternally, &c.,

FRANCIS D. CLARK,
Formerly of Co. D.

No. 38 CORTLAND STREET,
NEW YORK, August 1st, 1883.

ADDITIONAL SURVIVORS.

Co. "A."

*CHIPMAN, WALTER .. .. .. Cedar Springs, Kent Co., Mich.
IRWIN, EDWARD .. .. Middleton, Lake Co., Cal.
*TAIT, JAMES A. .. .. Santa Cruz, Cal.

Co. "B."

*GALLAGHER, JOHN .. Bodega Corner, Sonoma Co., Cal.
WEISS, WILLIAM .. .. San Francisco.

Co. "C."

*LIEUT. THERON R. PER LEE .. .. Baltimore, Md.
ZETSCHSKY, CHARLES .. .. Petaluma, Cal.

Co. "D."

*JANES, ALDEN W. .. .. Kenton, Hardin Co., Ohio.

Co. "E."

*BAXTER, WILLIAM O. .. .. Santa Monica, Cal.

Co. "F."

LOPEZ, THEODORE .. .. .. Sonora, Toulumne Co., Cal.
*MILFORD, EDMUND N. .. .. .. Princeton, Mariposa Co., Cal.

Co. "G."

*GROW, WILLIAM .. .. Deadwood, Dakota Ter.
GEHRINGER, ANDREW .. .. .. Concord, Contra Costa Co., Cal.

Co. "I."

LUKER, WILLIAM .. .. .. Sonora, Tuolumne Co., Cal.

Co. "K."

FRINK, DANIEL . .. .. Mountain View, Santa Clara Co., Cal.
*LEACH, KENDRICK N. .. Fountain Green, Hancock Co., Ill.
LOVELAND, CYRUS C. .. .. Santa Clara Co., Cal.

Regimental Band.

DUNITCH, ERNEST F. .. .. near Placerville, Cal.
*HAUFF, ERNEST .. .. .. Yorkville, Mendocino Co., Cal.

*Information direct from themselves.

DEATHS—1882 AND '83.

Co. "A."

LEWIS, JOSEPH B.	Fort Davis, Texas, June 24, 1882
BOUCHALTZ, THEODORE	near Mariposa, Cal., June 11, 1883.

Co. "D."

ATKINSON, CHARLES A.	Mariposa, Cal., August 7, 1882.
HILL, JOHN EVANS	Pendelton, Oregon, August 6, 1882.
SCHREADOR, GEORGE	Napa Co., Cal., Sept. 20, 1882.

Co. "G."

LIEUT. JEREMIAH SHERWOOD,	New York City, March 14, 1883.

"Co. J."

OSGOOD, HENRY M.	San Luis Obispo, Cal., Dec. 9, 1882.
GUIBAL, EUGENE	Gilroy, Cal., ——— 1883.

Co. "K."

MERRITT, ROBERT G.	Ukiah, Mendocino Co., March 27, 1883.

Additional information received—Deaths.

Co. "A."

BURKE, JAMES	on Stanislaus river, ——, 1851.
DENKERS, CHARLES W.	at Sacramento, May 4, 1871.
HATHAWAY, JAMES M.	at Downieville, Sierra Co., ——, 1851.
HAMILTON, JAMES	at Jackson, Amador Co., ——, 1858.
MORTON, FREEMAN	at Stockton, Cal., ——, 185-.
MORSE, HENRY	on San Joaquin Plains, ——, 1849.
MURRAY, EDWARD	in Calaveras Co., ——, 1855.
PENROSE, LIEUT. GEO. F.	at Monterey, Cal., ——, 185-.
PEASLEY, NESMITH H.	at San Francisco, ——, 1851.
SCHOONMAKER, MILTON C.	at Stockton, Cal., Jan'y —, 1850.
SCHILLER, EDWARD	at ——, Texas, ——, 1881.
TAIT, WILLIAM G.	at ——, Nic., ——, 185-.
TIPSON, WILLIAM H.	at San Francisco, Dec. 7, 1867.

Co. "B."

BRADY, JOHN R.	at Stockton, Cal., ——, 185-.
FITCH, WORTHINGTON L.	at San Francisco, ——, 1850.

OGDEN, BENJAMIN .. .. .. at Brooklyn, N. Y., Nov. —, 1866.
PECK, CHARLES L. .. at Monterey, Cal., ——, 1854.
RYAN, EDWARD .. .. at San Francisco, ——, 1866.
RANDALL, CHARLES G. .. at San Jose, Cal., ——, 185-.
RICHARDSON, CHARLES .. .. at sea, brig "Vesta." ——, 1855.
SCOTT, CHARLES G. .. .. .. at ——, Nic., ——, 185-.
TOWNER, LOAMMI .. .. at San Jose, Cal. ——, 185-.
WALL, RICHARD .. .. at Linden, San Joaquin Co., ——, 185-.

Co. "C."

LAYDEN, WILLIAM .. .. .. at Sandwich Islands, ——, 185-.

Co. "D."

REASSEAU, CHARLES .. .. at San Francisco, ——, 1868.
WILSON, JOHN .. . at Firebaughs Ferry, Cal., ——, 1870.
WARRINGTON, JOHN at Indian Reservation, Mendocino Co., ——185-.

Co. "E."

CAMPBELL, JAMES T. .. .. .. at San Francisco, ——, 1853.
KIERNAN, JOHN B. .. .. .. at Stockton, Cal., ——, 186-.
LEGARE, BURNETT .. .. at Sea, ——. 1866.
McPHERSON, GEORGE .. at Morrisania, N. Y., Feb. 20, 1869.
McMANUS, JAMES .. .. at San Francisco, ——, 1852.
McMILLAN, CHARLES " " ——, 186-.
MORTON, HENRY S. .. .. at Stockton, Cal., ——, 1854.
VERMULE, LIEUT. THOMAS L. .. at Stockton, Cal., May 7, 1856.
MILLIKEN, JOHN .. .. .. at Santa Clara Co. (about), 1878.
HUTCHEON, WALTER .. .. at Brooklyn, N. Y., Feb. 15, 1880.
VAN RIPER, ABRAHAM (Sergt.) on Mokelumne River, Winter of 1848-'49.

Co. "F."

CARPENTER, CHARLES R. .. .. at Havana, Cuba, ——, 1860.
GALUSHA, ELON A. .. .. at Rochester, N. Y., ——, 18-.
MASON, ALFRED .. .. at Sacramento, ——, 18-.
MULVEY, JAMES at San Francisco, ——, 1865.
PULIS, JOHN C. .. " " ——, 1850.
POWER, EDWARD " " ——, 185-.
POWER, JOHN A. .. .. .. at Sonora, Mexico, ——, 1860.
SMITH, JAMES G. { Drowned at Middle Fork of the American River. Cal., ——, 1849.
STEPHENS, PETER, ... at San Francisco, ——, 1849.
VIDAL, JOHN A. .. at Santa Barbara. ——, 1853.

Co. "G."

FARR, PHILIP .. .. at Dutch Flat, Cal., ——, 18-.
TOYE, H. H. F. at Granada, Nic., ——, 1856.

Co. "G."

DAVIS, BENJAMIN B.	..	at Merced, Cal., ——, 1880.
LEDDY, MICHAEL	..	Mendocino County, ——, 18—.
VEDDER, PETER G.	.. ..	at Manaque, Nic., ——, 1856.
WIERZBICKIE, FELIX P.	..	at San Francisco, Dec. 25, 1860.

Co. "J."

KELLY, PHILIP .. .. in Calaveras Co., ——, 1860.

Co. "K."

DIMMICK, CAPT. K. H.	..	at Los Angeles, Sept. 11, 1861.
GRAMS, PHILIP	.. ..	at Milwaukee, Wis., ——, 1880.

Regimental Band.

FAUFTER, JOHANN .. .. at Washington, D. C., ——, 1864.

Sutler.

HAIGHT, SAMUEL W. at San Francisco, Feb. 27, 1856.

ERRATA.—(See Volume.)

Folio 22—CAPT. J. L. FOLSOM, read .. .. 19th instead of 15th.
" 22—ROBERT MURRAY, Assistant Surgeon, U. S. A., was not an an officer of the regiment, but served at various posts in California, garrisoned by the regiment. His present rank is Colonel and Assistant Surgeon-General, U. S. A. Stationed at Fort Columbus, Governor's Island, staff of Gen. W. S. Hancock, U. S. A.
" 25—CHARLES W. DENKERS, .. See deaths in Appendix.
" 26—THEODORE BONCHALTZ, read THEODORE BOUCHALTZ.
" 28—JAMES DRENNER, read JAMES DRENNEN
" 31—ARTEMUS RICHARDSON, read Sonora, Tuolumne Co.
" 33—CHARLES REASSEAU, See deaths in Appendix.
" 33—JAMES M. HARRON, read JAMES HARRON.
" 34—ALDEN W. JAMES, read .. ALDEN W. JANES.
" 34—GEORGE SCHRAELOR, read .. GEORGE SCHREADOR.
" 39—JAMES DOULEVY, read .. .. JAMES DONLEVY.
" 44—JAMES F. GORDWELL, read .. JAMES F. GOODWELL.
" 48—FREDERICK N. LEACH, read KENDRICK N. LEACH.

Names reported *which do not appear on the official roll* of the regiment. Some of the members of the regiment enlisted under assumed names to avoid discovery by parents and guardians, and resumed their proper names upon the discharge of the regiment in 1848. This may account for some of these names reported.

BROWN, WILLIAM H.
BRUEN, JOHN H.
BENSON, CHRISTIAN
CONLEY, MARSTON F.
CUNNINGHAM, STEPHEN
CASSEL, JOHN
CHRISTIAN, CHARLES
DAY, EDWARD
FORD, HENRY
HAWKINS, JOHN A.
HOFFMAN, CHARLES
HEATHCOAT, ———
HARRISON, LIEUT. EDW. H.
KORN, JULIUS

KORNISH, ———
LIGHT, JAMES
MAST, HERMAN
McDUFF, A. JACKSON
McDONALD, CHARLES
McGLOENE, JAMES
McLEOD, ALEXANDER
O'GRADY, ———
PARSONS, J. H
RAND, GEORGE
SMITH JOHN G. (James G. in Co. F.)
WALTER, JOHN
YETCH, AUGUST

Information received of Comrades.

Co. A.—PENNY, MOSES H. .. .. Went to Chili, S. C., in 1850.
" K.—MAC KAY, JOHN H. — San Francisco, Cal.
" A.—NOYES, MICHAEL S. — Unionville, Humboldt Co., Nev.
" B.—WHITE, CRISTOPHER S. — Silver City, Lyon Co., Idaho.
" D.—CAHN, PHILIP V. — Oakland, Cal.
" E.—HAMLEN, MORTIMER J. Said to be living at — San Francisco, Cal.
" E.—BURTON, JAMES C. — Los Angeles, Cal.
" G.—EDMONSON, ALFRED — San Francisco, Cal.
" G.—TAYLOR, WALTER — Corpus Christie, Texas.
" I.—BROOKS, EDWARD J. — Muscogee, Creek Nation, I. T.

P. S.—*The effort made to verify the above was unsuccessful.*

Survivors of the 100 members of the regiment that arrived in California by the transport "Isabella," under Lieut. Thomas J. Roach:

AMES, JOSIAH P.
CORGAN, GEORGE A.
CHANDLER, JOHN A.
CLARK, FRANCIS D.
CLAMP, RICHARD
FARLEY, GEORGE
FARLEY, THOMAS P.
HAVEY, JOHN
JANES, ALDEN W.

LIPP, CARLOS
NORRIS, JACOB W.
PHILLIPS, JOHN B.
RUSS, C. C. E.
SIMS, JOSEPH
THOMAS, JOHN W.
TAIT, JAMES A.
TOOMBS, GEORGE W.
WILLIAMS, WILLIAM H.

CONTRIBUTORS TO THE PUBLICATION FUND.

FIELD AND STAFF, $25.

COL. J. D. STEVENSON.   CAPT. W. G. MARCY, Commissary.
LIEUT. J. C. BONNYCASTLE, Adjutant.

Co. A—$18.

EDWARD BARTHROP,
RUSSELL MYERS,
JOHN B. PARVIN,
MOSES W. PERRY,
WILLIAM H. ROGERS,
JOHN SCOLLAN,
JAMES THOMPSON,
JOHN W. THOMAS,
WILLIAM WOOLEY,
WILLIAM H. WILLIAMS

Co. B—$24.

LIEUT. THOS. E. KETCHUM.
JOSIAH P. AMES,
SAMUEL CATTS,
CHARLES HEINRICH,
ANDREW J. MOORE,
CHARLES H. THURSTON.

Co. C—$15.

LIEUT. THERON R. PER LEE,
ADOLPH P. RUSS.

Co. D—$33.

GEORGE A. CORGAN,
GEORGE C. DEAN,
JAMES HARRON,
WILLIAM S. JOHNSON,
ALDEN W. JANES,
JACOB W. NORRIS,
WILLIAM D. ROBINSON,
JOSEPH SIMS,
JOHN WOLFE,
ALPHIAS YOUNG.

Co. E—$26.

CAPT. NELSON TAYLOR,
LIEUT. EDWARD WILLIAMS.
WILLIAM BAXTER,
WILLIAM BOYERS,
GEORGE CANFIELD,
ISAAC C. JOHNSON,
JOHN M. O'NEIL,
JOHN H. WELSH.

Co. F—$33.

CAPT. FRANCIS J. LIPPITT,
AUGUST ENGELBERG,
JAMES LYNCH,
AUGUST RUSS,
C. C. E. RUSS,
AMISON WHITAKER.

Co. G—$37.

LIEUT. J. Mc. H. HOLLINGS-
    WORTH,
LIEUT. J. SHERWOOD,
THOMAS NISBITT,
E. D. SHIRLAND,
ADOLPH PFIESTER,
ROBERT WILSON.

Co. H—$28.

CAPT. JOHN B. FRISBIE,
JAMES A. LAPPEUS,
SQUIRE G. MERRILL,
GEORGE VAN VECHTEN.

Co. I—$24.

JOSEPH EVANS,
JOHN C. EMERSON,
EUGENE GUIBAL,
H. M. OSGOOD,
ELIJAH M. SMITH,
CORNELIUS SULLIVAN,
ANDREW J. WARD.

Co. K.

....

Non-Members of Regiment—$26.

JOHN Q. ADAMS,	BENJ. W. JENNESS,
THEODORE RUSS,	HON. PHILIP A. ROACH,
W. C. OSBORNE,	C. A. MARTELLS.

While it would have afforded great pleasure to have made special mention of those comrades who so generously came to the aid and assistance of the publication fund, I abstain from so doing, feeling that many who contributed gave to the extent of their ability, and that a discrimination would be unjust to those, who, while their means were limited, yet cheerfully gave of that little, when *other comrades, with ample means, declined or neglected to contribute*. The total expense that will have been incurred with the issue of the Appendix amounts to $400; of this amount $290 has been received as follows: *One* contributed $20, *eight* $10 each, one $7, *twenty-four* $5 each, *four* $3 each, *four* $2.50 each, *fourteen* $2 each, and *thirteen* $1 each.

To provide for the deficiency, copies of this volume, with the Appendix bound therein, will be furnished at $2 each, or three copies for $5. Those who have contributed to the publication fund will receive the Appendix sheets (which are uniform with those in the volume) free of charge.

WHAT IS SAID OF THE "LITTLE VOLUME."

"WASHINGTON, D. C., July 1, 1882.

"I thank you truly for the handsome volume, entitled, 'The First Regiment of New York Vols., 1846-1882,' compiled and issued by you. Few of the men who composed that regiment are living to appreciate the graceful tribute to their memory, but they left families and hosts of friends who will be delighted to possess in a small compass so many names, and the history of so many events with which that regiment was associated. In casting my eyes over the volume I find names that were once familiar, and am reminded of things lost to all but memory. I congratulate you on your success, and beg to subscribe myself as one of your friends." W. T. SHERMAN, General.

"Your valuable work came duly to hand, and I am really delighted with its neatness and beauty of finish. Its contents are just what they should be. Accept my thanks for the courtesy and kind attention you have ever shown your old commander, and believe me, most sincerely and truly, your friend,"

J. D. STEVENSON, Colonel (of the Regiment).

"Your book has given me great pleasure, and I am thankful to you for all the labor and trouble you have expended on the records of our old regiment. Many familiar names come to my mind again from thirty-five years ago. It a very nice book to hand over to our children when we are called away."

A. PFIESTER, Co. G.

"I am much pleased with the external of the book; its neat and attractive appearance commends itself. With regard to its contents, I think those in sympathy with your undertaking have good reason to be more than satisfied, for you have given them more than they expected. Its arrangement is admirable, and the object you had in mind in its production is well and fully covered, and in good taste.

"I know you have spent a great deal of labor and thought in its preparation and production, but feel assured that you will consider yourself well paid for the labor and time expended, in the congratulation of friends, and the favor I am confident it will be received by our comrades of the old regiment."

NELSON TAYLOR, Capt. Co. E.

"A more welcome book has never made its appearance in my house, not only to myself, but my family." JAMES LYNCH, Co. F.

"Your little volume relating to our old regiment is to hand. I am much pleased with it. Only for your zeal and devotion we would have passed into oblivion. I shall treasure it as an heir-loom for my two orphan granddaughters." JOHN SCOLLAN, Co. A.

"CITY OF MEXICO, Nov. 22, 1882.

"It affords me much pleasure to have an opportunity of expressing my high appreciation of the service you have rendered to your old comrades in thus preserving the memory of our regiment." JOHN B. FRISBIE, Capt. Co. H.

"I have your beautiful book relating to our old regiment. The great labor which you must have given the subject is worthy of the highest reward your old comrades can bestow." WILLIAM C. PARKER, Ass't Surgeon.

"The thanks of this Society are tendered Mr. Francis D. Clark, for a copy of his work, which we highly appreciate." JOHN C. ROBINSON, Sec'y,
Associated Veterans of the Mexican War, San Francisco.

"Your little volume reads to me like a roll-call, and carries my thoughts back thirty-six years, when the most of us were mere youths, among whom I remember you well." GEORGE CANFIELD, Co. E.

"I have read with deep interest your book, and you deserve much credit for energy and perseverance in getting it up, and I can thoroughly appreciate the difficulties under which you labored in order to avoid giving offense to any one."

J. McH. HOLLINGSWORTH, Lieut. Co. G.

"A very creditable work, and affords me great satisfaction in accounting for many of my old comrades, of whom, while I regret the dead, am glad to see so many are certainly alive." JOHN C. BONNYCASTLE, Lieut. and Adjt.

"It is a valuable work, and splendidly gotten up."

PHILIP A. ROACH, of San Francisco.

"The book is exceedingly creditable in every respect."
SEYMOUR G. STEELE (Captain), Co. A.

"The book is very valuable, and I will treasure it as a keepsake of old days never to be forgotten."
GEORGE VAN VECHTEN, Co. H.

"We all owe you a debt for your labor and perseverance. Accept my heartfelt thanks."
ANDREW J. MOORE, Co. A.

"I cannot refrain from congratulating you on its very handsome typographical and general appearance, not to speak of its valuable information."
JOHN C. EMERSON, Co. I.

"I am intensely pleased, and prize it highly. The survivors owe you a debt of gratitude."
JOHN B. PARVIN, Co. A.

"Just the information I most desired." E. D. SHIRLAND, Co. G.

"The book is admirable in make up, and is an interesting and valuable record. Your enterprise is creditable, and a gracious tribute to the veterans."
JOHN Q. ADAMS, son of JAMES H. ADAMS, Co. G.

"You deserve great credit and thanks for the zeal displayed in our behalf. I very much doubt if any other man would have undertaken to perpetuate the memories of the dear old regiment."
SQUIRE G. MERRILL, Co. H.

"I am instructed to convey to you the thanks of this Society for your gift, as also to assure you of its appreciation of your valuable work, and the gratitude expressed by many at its compilation."
WILLIAM G. FREEMAN, Sec'y,
San Joaquin Society of California Pioneers, Stockton, Cal.

"Many thanks for your efforts in furnishing the valuable information your work contains. It afforded me a rich treat in renewing my memory of old times and the boys of '46–'48, of which by far the greater proportion are enrolled with the silent majority."
GEO. N. CORNWELL, Co. H.

"I am satisfied that every one connected with the regiment owes you a volume of thanks, and I hasten to return you mine." J. C. L. WADSWORTH.

"I am highly pleased, and feel thankful to you for the publication of such a splendid work."
JAMES H. ADAMS, Co. G.

The following letter, received from a comrade, shows that the old time feeling of generosity has not departed from the early pioneers of California, which, under the circumstances, is a liberal offering:

FRIEND CLARK, New York City: TUCSON, ARIZONA, Feb. 25, 1883.

Enclosed please find P. O. order for three dollars to help defray the expense of printing the handsome volume received. Not being rich, I am obliged to labor for my daily bread, so cannot do better for you.
M. W. PERRY, Co. A.

1848.] REUNION AT NEW YORK. [1882.

Wednesday Evening, Oct. 24, 1882.

Thirty-fourth anniversary of the discharge of the last company (D) of the regiment from service at Monterey, Cal.

The following account of the gathering of survivors of Stevenson's California Expedition on the above evening, is taken from the *New York Herald*, of the following morning:

MEXICAN WAR VETERANS.

ANNIVERSARY DINNER OF **THE MEN WHO ANTIDATE** THE FORTY-NINERS.

Each one of a company of gentlemen who sat down last evening to dinner at Martinelli's wore a little gold figure of a bear on his breast. This is an insignia worn only by pioneers who preceded the Forty-niners to California. The party of diners were the veterans of the First regiment of New York Volunteers of the Mexican war. The regiment was raised by order of President Polk, with orders to proceed to California by the then only method—around Cape Horn. Colonel Jonathan D. Stevenson was placed in command, and the instructions of the regiment were to take possession of the Mexican province of California and hold it. President Polk, looking to the future benefit of the province, gave instructions that the material of the regiment should be carefully chosen and as far as possible should consist of young unmarried men with trades. There was quite a competition to get into the regiment, and many of the best families of this State were represented in the thousand men and officers who set sail on September 26, 1846, in the transports Thomas H. Perkins, Loo Choo, Susan Drew and other craft. The trip was a long and eventful one, the entire winter of 1846-7 being spent in making the voyage. The several South American ports were stopped at, and some very remarkable pranks were played by the young soldier lads. There were a few lives lost by heavy storms about Cape Horn, but the vessels arrived at San Francisco in good shape in March, 1847. The bulk of the work of conquering the province had already been accomplished by the naval forces, but the regiment found plenty to do in keeping order and in performing garrison duty; and it was not until October 24, 1848, that the last wing of the regiment was disbanded and the several members settled down to civil avocations.

The discovery of gold brought on the rush of fortune-seekers. These later comers wear the badge of the silver bear, and proudly refer to themselves as pioneers; but the First regiment veterans were already on the spot.

AROUND THE FESTIVE BOARD.

The dinner last evening was held on the date of the disbandment of the command, and was attended by such of the old members as had drifted back in the course of years to New York. Among those present were William H. Rogers, Russell Myers and William H. Williams, of Company A; James E. Nuttman and Charles J. McPherson, of Company B; Francis D. Clark, John Wolfe and Jacob W. Norris, of Company D; John H. Welsh, of Company E; Lieutenant Jeremiah Sherwood, of Company G; George Van Vechten, of Company H; Joseph Evans and Frank S. Stuart, of Company I. Major Clark presided, and the evening was spent in recalling incidents—pathetic, humorous and valuable—as historic material. All sorts of escapades in various South American ports were confessed to, and many bits of insight into the quaint ways of the native and immigrant population of early California were told. During the dinner Roswell D. Baldwin, the second officer of the Loo Choo, entered the room and was heartily welcomed. He had seen a notice of the meeting and had not before known of the organization of the Gold Bear Veterans. Later in the evening letters were read from absent members and from the parent organization of the regiment's veterans in California.

The following telegram was received from the venerable Colonel of the regiment at San Francisco:

"*Comrades assembled at New York:*

"On my bended knees I ask God's blessing on you all.

"JONATHAN D. STEVENSON."

The memory of dead comrades was duly honored and many speeches of congratulation over the growth of the State which each one present had assisted in establishing were made. After midnight there were many empty bottles and some wonderful efforts in talking Mexican Spanish from memory.

Gen'l Edward O. C. Ord, United States Army, died at Havana, Cuba, Sunday evening, July 22, 1883, of yellow fever. In 1847-8 he was a Lieutenant of Co. F, 3d U. S. Artillery, and was stationed at Monterey, Cal. Members of Stevenson's regiment will remember this officer—especially those of Co. "D" and "I," with whom his duties were so closely identified during their term of service in California.

AN INTERESTING REMINISCENCE.

THE FOURTH OF JULY AT LOS ANGELES IN 1847.

First celebration of the glorious anniversary of our National Independence, in California, by order of Col. Stevenson; the Stars and Stripes unfurled from the heights of Los Angeles.

Head-quarters Southern Military District,

Ciudad De Los Angeles, July 2d, 1847.

Order No. 1.—The anniversary of the birthday of American Independence will be celebrated at this port in a manner as worthy of the occasion as our means will admit, and if we cannot greet its return by a display of as much pomp and ceremony as will no doubt be made at many ports within our own native land, we will be unsurpassed by a proper demonstration of that pure heart-felt joy, which should animate the heart of every lover of freedom and free institutions throughout the civilized world upon the happy return of this glorious day.

At sunrise a Federal salute will be fired from the field-work on the hill, which commands this town, and for the first time from this point the American standard is displayed.

At 10 o'clock every soldier at this post will be under arms. The detachment of the Seventh Regiment of N. Y. Volunteers and the first Regiment of U. S. Dragoons (dismounted), will be marched to the field-work on the hill, under the command of their respective senior officers present, when, together with the Mormon Battalion, the whole will be formed at 11 o'clock A. M. into a hollow square, when the Declaration of Independence will be read.

At the close of this ceremony, the field-works will be dedicated and appropriately named, and at 12 o'clock a national salute will be fired, which will close the ceremonies of the day.

Lieutenant Smith commanding detachment of U. S. Dragoons, will cause a proper detail to be made from his command to fire the salute.

The field-work at this post, having been planned, and the work conducted entirely by A. A. Quarter-Master Davidson of the 1st Regiment Dragoons, he is requested to hoist upon it, for the first time, on the morning of the Fourth, the American standard.

It is the custom of our country to confer on its fortifications the name of some distinguished individual, who has rendered important services to his country, either in the councils of the nation or on the battle-field. The Commandant has therefore determined, unless the Department of War shall otherwise direct, to confer upon the field-work, erected at the port of Los Angeles, the name of one who was regarded, by all who had the pleasure of his acquaintance, as a perfect specimen of an American officer, and whose character, for every virtue and accomplishment that adorns a gentleman, was only equalled by the reputation he had acquired in the field for his gallantry as an officer and soldier, and his life was sacrificed in the conquest of this territory at the battle of San Pasqual. The Commander directs, that from and after the 4th instant, it shall bear the name of Moore.

Circumstances, over which we have no control, have prevented the command at this port being completely uniformed, but each officer and soldier will appear on the Fourth with the perfect equipments of his corps as f r as he has them, and most perfect cleanliness, as well in arms and accoutrements as in person, will be required of all. Each department will be minutely inspected before assembling on the hill. By order of

COL. J. D. STEVENSON,

J. C. BONNYCASTLE,

First Lieut. and Adjt.

www.ingramcontent.com/pod-product-compliance
Lightning Source LLC
Chambersburg PA
CBHW021945160426
43195CB00011B/1229